CW01460841

MAKE THAT 17...
HAPPY TRAILS
xxx

CONTENTS

AUTHOR'S NOTE:

What you are about to read is a true story. Well, it's true enough. In May of 2019 I flew down to Cusco, Peru and took a guided trek to Machu Picchu.

When I returned I spoke, online and on the phone, with three others who had done the same sort of trek at roughly the same time. I spoke with each of them, three people from different backgrounds and regions, rather extensively. Their stories then became my stories. The most interesting people from their treks joined my trek. In short, our four separate treks have become one.

The characters who you will read about are again "real enough." All of the names have been changed. Some are from my trek, others are from the treks of people I spoke with once I was home. Most are actually a combination of two or three different people. One is a girl whom I met while backpacking around Europe years ago. I wanted her on the trek, so she joined us in my imagination. It works.

You may get the feeling that I disliked some of the people on my trip. I did not. Few of us would naturally hang out with each other if not thrust together like this, but all fifteen of my hiking companions were good people.

I did decide to leave one name the same. Rosel Calderon Mollehuanca, aka "Super Hiker." He was our guide for the trip and he was truly excellent. To honor him, his real name appears in this book. Please do understand that not all of the words and thoughts that are attributed to Rosel in this book are actually his. I have used him as a vehicle to tell the history of Peru, the Inca people, the trail, and of course Machu Picchu itself. I have tried to stay true to his spirt at all times. (If I have said anything that you would not actually say, Rosel, I apologize.) I have also thrown spelling and grammar out the window and written Rosel how he actually sounds. For a non-native speaker, he speaks quite well.

You will notice that I am not a professor of history or anthropology at an Ivy League college. I'm also not a professor at a community college. I'm just a dude who went to Machu Picchu, nothing more. I happen to think that I have a good ear, the writer's gift for dialog, and a solid sense of humor. I hope you'll agree. If I know a little bit more about this subject than you do, it is only because I read a bit to prep for this book. Quite a few of you are likely more versed on the subject than I am.

If you're looking for a textbook to really dig deeply into the Inca culture, the history of Machu Picchu, and the evolution of the modern sub species of llamas, this ain't it. Put this rag down and go buy a real book.

What you are holding is a humorous travelogue, it is a short and easy read. This is the reality of what it is like to actually hike the pathways of the Incas exactly how they did six-hundred years ago, assuming they had porters running ahead of them to set up their tents, cook their meals, clean their toilets, administer oxygen, remind them to put on sunscreen, and pose them for pictures. It is an account of sixteen realistic first-world tourists on a quest for social-media photos. In between humorous anecdotes I will attempt to, quickly, slip in a little history. Don't worry, you'll hardly feel it.

"Joel, best wishes as you continue with your adventures"

-Robert Redford

CHAPTER 1: MICHIGAN

"So I grabbed the alligator by the back of the tail."

"This is nuts," Kim said. She was my date to a dinner party which I was now monopolizing with tales from last summer's adventures. I wrote a book, *A Man, A Mustang, and the United States of America,* where I chronicled my journey in a 1967 Mustang convertible while participating in five extreme adventures.

I began by living with some really nice gear heads in Ohio. We rebuilt a 1984 Cadillac, then I drove it in a demolition derby. Next, I went down to Florida and learned alligator wrestling from some Seminole Indians. Later I would compete in the MR340, the longest kayak race in the world, and the Midnight Run, a 90-mile dog-sled race across the frozen Upper Peninsula of Michigan. Oh, and I also trained as a bull rider under Gary Lafew, the 1976 world bull-riding champion, then rode three bulls and did a little rodeo clowning.

"So wait," Ben cut in. He was a software engineer who once went scuba diving for a whole hour while at a resort in Mexico. "You're grabbing an alligator by the tail?"

"Yeah."

"But isn't this with the same hand that you injured while bull riding?"

"It was, and that proved to be a problem."

"This is nuts," Kim said again.

"Don't people lose hands this way?" Ben sat with his mouth open, one of those way too hard, half cookies, half biscuits, the kind that nobody really likes but they always show up at dinner parties, hanging from his mouth.

"Well I don't know about hands," I said. "But the guy who

was training me did only have two fingers."

"Absolutely nuts."

"Yeah but it turns out that he cut them off in an accident with a chain saw, so I felt pretty good about that. Plus, he had a stick to pry the gator's mouth open if he happened to get me, so he seemed pretty official."

"How long was this kayak race again?"

"340 miles. I tore my left rotator cuff somewhere around mile 270 so the final 70 or so miles were a real pain."

"And you... 340 miles! How much time did that take you?"

"I finished in seventy-seven hours."

"How do you sleep?"

"Well you don't really. I slept a total of six hours, the rest of the time I was just paddling. Thing is, you start to hallucinate in the boat on the second night, happens to everyone. I ended up barking at a tree because I thought it looked like a poodle. I mean it really did look like a poodle."

"So you paddle at night?"

"Paddle all the time, the race never stops."

"And the dog sled race, how did you not get lost in the woods?"

"You trust the dogs."

"The dogs?"

"Sure, they know what they're doing, I'm the tourist. As far as they're concerned, I'm just 170 pounds of shit."

Matt's wife, Heidi, who never did like me, started to make a comment. Something about the dogs being right, I'm sure. Instead she just smirked, then she proceeded to daintily dunk an overpriced cookie in her tea in a manner that she would never do if it weren't for the fact that others were watching her, approving of her *Downton Abby*-like manners. She may not have spoken aloud, but her eyes clearly told me that I was once again ruining her dinner party.

I'll be honest, I did bring a twelve-pack of craft beer and a bag of soft-batch cookies simply because I knew how much it would annoy her. But it should also be noted that they were the first things to go.

Along the same lines I'm sure that she also was not too fond of Kim, my date. Not that there was anything wrong with Kim, quite the opposite.

"How old is she?" Matt mumbled out of the side of his mouth when we were somewhat alone.

"23," I shot back in a half whisper.

He looked left, looked right, then quickly gave me an under-the-table fist bump before he was ordered to serve the crackers and cheese.

"Wasn't it cold?" Ben asked me. A few months ago he had told the group that it did get chilly on his one-hour scuba dive in Mexico. They only gave him a short-sleeve wet suit.

"Wind chill brought it down to negative thirty."

"Holy malarkey!" He then proceeded to laugh like a donkey trying to catch its breath.

"I wore two pair of long johns, winter hiking pants, and snow overalls. Same on top, two pair of long johns, a sweater, a light jacket, then a huge jacket over it all. When I got to the first check point, I was just about frozen to death."

"Well, we all have stories." Heidi cut me off with a practiced smile that didn't suit her face.

But Matt, a big fan of 80s rock who was entirely sick of the light jazz that he and his wife *mutually* agreed on for these game nights, was having none of it. "Hang on. I want to hear about this demolition derby!"

"The scariest part honestly wasn't driving. Once you smash into someone, and get crashed into, you really calm down and just get to the business at hand. The toughest part was actually the demolition derby right before mine."

"How so?"

"So there's twenty of us, we're up next, just sitting in our cars right outside of the arena while the heat before ours is going. We can't see anything, but you can hear everything. I mean you can feel it man! The crashes move the earth under you, and the roar of the crowd comes a split second after, like the thunder following the lightning when it's way too close to your house! It felt like that scene from *Gladiator* where Russell Crowe is waiting for his turn to go into the arena and do battle."

"That's amazing."

"So, I have Scrabble, Trivial Pursuit, or Pictionary."

"Two cars went up in flames. We couldn't see them, we just hear the horns, hear the fire hoses spraying them down, and hope that nobody is getting burnt alive."

Ben allowed guacamole dip to drop on his shirt as he listened intently. His wife clucked her tongue and rolled her eyes while she proceeded to wet a napkin and clean his shirt like he was a three-year-old.

"You're seriously crazy!" Kim said again with a smile that could not hide how much she loved it.

'So Kim." Heidi turned her practiced smile to her. "I understand you're in a sorority? That must be fun."

"What about the bull riding?" Ben asked as his wife continued to dip her napkin in his water glass and clean his shirt.

"You remember when you were in high school and you and your buddies would drive your car onto a frozen lake to do doughnuts?"

"No, I never did that!" Ben said, quickly followed by the donkey-trying-to-catch-his-breath laugh.

"Well, pretend that you had. Then pretend that instead of being inside the car you sit on the roof and try to hold on to the luggage rack while your buddy is spinning around like a madman."

"Wow."

"Only difference would be, when you eventually fly off of the roof of your car, your buddy isn't trying to run you over. The bull is."

Ben spilled more dip onto his shirt. His wife sighed. "Ok, this is coming off." Ben did as he was told and took off his shirt. Sitting at the table in a plain-white T he somehow managed to be both skinny and fat at the same time. A middle-aged man's pot belly sat under his twelve-year-old boy arms. He looked like a hundred and fifty pounds of chewed bubble gum.

"That's amazing," Eric told me. "I'd like to do something like that sometime."

"No, you wouldn't." His wife corrected him.

"No, I'm just saying I'd like to."

"Nope."

"Ok." He loaded some cheese onto a cracker.

"So, dude what are you doing next?" Matt asked and everyone stopped to look at me.

I remembered a conversation that I had years ago with an acquaintance who was a professional juggler. "The audience doesn't want to see you juggle five balls, six balls, or even seven balls," he had told me. "They want to see you juggle one more ball than you're capable of."

"Um, I don't know."

Everyone turned away. Heidi smirked at me smugly as all the attention turned to Pictionary.

****

I tried to sleep. I couldn't. All I saw was Heidi's smug face. I was boring again. Average. Ordinary. I was a middle-aged man in a one-bedroom apartment. I owned slippers. In the morning I would make a smoothie then bring out my laptop and get to work. I was Ben, minus the salary.

I looked into my closet, deep into the back of my closet. Trekking pants, boots, a lightweight cowboy-style explorer hat. An empty travel diary.

All night I entered absurd things into Google.

Wrestle a bear.

Ride on the space shuttle.

What would Superman do?

How to go on a real adventure that ends with you hanging onto the underside of a helicopter?

Camel trek across Mongolia.

Trek with llamas.

That's when it came up: Machu Picchu.

"What the heck is Machu Picchu?" I had heard of it. When I clicked on it I saw images and instantly recognized the classic photo pointed down at the ruins with the mountains behind them.

I went over to Wikipedia.

"Machu Picchu is a 15th century Inca citadel, located in the Eastern Cordillera of southern Peru." Sounded alright so far.

"On an eight thousand foot mountain ridge." Ok, now we're talking.

"It is located in the Cusco region, blah, blah, blah, something about a Sacred Valley, some Umba something or other river…"

"Many people experience extreme altitude sickness." Those are normal people, not me.

"One of the seven wonders of the world." Ok, I like that.

"Hey Joel, have you seen any of the wonders of the world?" I pictured people at Heidi's dinner parties asking me.

"Quite a few of them. Ancient or modern?" I would answer. From somewhere behind me movie theme music would play. Peru, yes, I liked this idea.

You could ride a train, or a bus, to Machu Picchu. Or you could get there the real way, by walking the ancient paths laid down by the Inca empire. I looked up a few of the companies that specialized in group treks to Machu Picchu. They all highlighted things like, "climb the mountains," "see history," "learn about the southern stars," "five days of intense but beautiful hiking."

It all sounded good, but I wasn't a hundred percent in yet. I kept reading.

"One of the seven wonders of the world, Machu Picchu was discovered in 1911 by Hiram Bingham, the man who inspired the character Indiana Jones."

If I'd owned a bullwhip I would have thrown it into my suitcase right then and there. I was sold.

CHAPTER 2: CUSCO

Detroit to Dallas:

My first leg was a four-hour flight. I didn't want to sleep yet, so I brought some food on the plane and plugged in my headphones. Over the course of the next four hours I watched two Matt Damon movies. I'm quite sure I've never said that sentence before in my life. First Matt Damon was an astronaut stranded on Mars. Next Matt Damon was shrunk to a few inches tall and living in a bubble community with other tiny people.

I of course could have used my time to read a guidebook on Peru and Machu Picchu, but who has time for that when there's so much accessibility to Matt Damon?

"Heading down to Dallas?" The man next to me asked. He looked like he had been shoved into his seat by a trash compactor then vacuum sealed.

The plane was going to Dallas, so I wasn't quite sure how else to answer.

"Yep."

"Yeah, me too." Again, the plane was flying to Dallas. "What are you doing down there?"

"It's just a stopover for me. I'm heading to Lima."

"Lima? Sounds like a bean."

"It's a city in Peru."

"Peru? Well I'll be! Going to a resort I take it?"

"Ah no, I'm hiking across the mountains to get to Machu Picchu."

"Gesundheit!" He laughed. Custom dictated that I give him a small smile and a very brief chuckle.

"It's one of the seven wonders of the world. The lost Incan city."

"Well I'll be!" he said again. "I'd like to do something like that someday."

Someday means never. He would never hike to Machu Picchu. He would never do anything like it.

I was not a someday kind of guy. I was a today kind of guy. I was going to Peru today. If you're reading this book then I hope you are on a plane right now. I hope you are a today sort of person too.

****

Dallas to Lima:

I had the worst seat in the house. 43 E, the middle seat, of the middle row, of the last row of the airplane.

"Son of a bitch," I mumbled as I made my way to the seat.

But then the plane began to fill up. There was no one to my left. There was no one to my right. Thus far I had three full seats to myself!

This couldn't last. Someone would come waddling down that aisle, likely reeking of cigarette smoke, and plop down next to me. But maybe only one more person would come? Maybe I would at least get one of the two aisle seats?

But my luck held out! Nobody came. The doors were shut, people were buckled in. I may have had the very back row of the plane, but it was all mine, three seats to stretch out on.

I moved to one of the aisle seats and buckled in.

"Sir, is this your seat?" The stewardess stood next to me.

"Well, technically this one is." I pointed to the middle seat. "But there's nobody here."

"May I see your boarding pass please?"

"Um, sure." I handed her my ticket.

"You're in 43 E."

"Yes."

"This is row 44."

"Huh?"

"This is your seat, one row up please."

I looked up one row. Not only was it the middle seat in a full plane, there was already a man sitting in it.

The stewardess saw the same thing. "Sir, may I see your boarding pass please?" She said to him.

"I'm actually two rows up, I was hoping to sit with my family."

The stewardess and I both looked up to see an open seat in 41 E.

"Sir, you can go to 41 E please."

"But, but can't I just stay here?"

"No, we use this row to rest."

I also wanted to rest. But, defeated, I got up.

"But maybe I can see if there are any other open seats?" she said to me.

"Please."

She pulled out a pocket device and looked at the layout of the plane. "You can go to row 21 sir, window seat."

"Perfect, thank you."

Row 21 was an exit row, there was enough leg room for anyone in the NBA. As soon as dinner was over, I leaned my seat back and slept the remaining four or five hours to Lima.

****

Lima to Cusco:

"Why are you coming to Peru?" The border agent glanced up at me.

"I'm hiking to Machu Picchu."

"Yes, and what is there?"

"Huh? It's one of the seven wonders of the world. I'm not exactly sure how to answer that question, thousands of people visit it every day."

"You go..." He then quickly rattled off some words, I believe in English, but with such an accent that it still sounded like he was speaking in Spanish.

"Wait, I, wha…"

"Next!"

I shuffled forward and got into a line with some other Americans. They also looked confused. Then a moron got into line right behind me. It made me feel good to be in a line, like I must somehow be in the right place. On the other hand, the moron was wearing pajama pants, a loose tank top, tie-dyed bandana, and a few months' worth of beard. Odds that he was carrying drugs seemed high to me. Odds that the boarder guards might think that he and I were traveling together seemed, well, possible.

The last thing I wanted was to end up in a Peruvian detention room with an Inca finger up my ass. I watched the moron put giant headphones on that allowed him to dance to music only he could hear while he sang every third or fourth word.

"Wrong line," a woman said to me after I'd been waiting for twenty minutes. "Next!"

"Wrong line? But where do I go?"

"Step aside please sir."

"But…"

"You go numeral ten please."

I walked, looking for the number ten.

There it was. I walked forward, passing a small man in a guard's uniform.

"No de esta manera."

"What?"

"No de esta manera."

"See I'm trying to get to number ten." I hold up two hands showing him all of my fingers. "Ten? Diez? Yo voy a la diez."

"Salir de esta manera, izquierda, va treinta metros, y usa esa puerta."

"Hang on a minute. I don't…" But he just said it faster and pointed me towards a door.

So I went through the door and stood on the sidewalk. I'm not even inside of the airport now, I thought to myself. I'm trying to catch a connecting flight from the sidewalk.

I walked back in and found another person. They had some sort of uniform on, looked official. "Diez? I was told to go to ten."

"Yes, this way. Outside, then back in through this door please."

"Ok, I'm already inside so it seems like it would be easier to just stay inside of the airport."

"No."

"So outside first then? Then back inside?"

"Si."

I ended up in the security line for the gate. I tried to explain to the guard at the beginning of the line that "I have just flown from Detroit to Dallas, they have already checked my bag. Then I flew from Dallas to Lima, and they also examined my bag. When I landed in Lima, here, aqui, you guys examined my bag. So the bag doesn't need more examining, comprendo?"

But he did not comprendo, he told me to wait in line.

"Sir I don't see my flight on the board."

"Como?"

"The board." I point to the board that says Salida/departures. "Me airoplane." I make my hand into a plane and fly it around, complete with plane noises like a three-year-old. "Me airoplane no es ahi."

"Ah, si! You no plane!"

"That's right. Yo no plane."

"Plane is canceled."

"Canceled? What do you mean canceled?"

"Es canceled."

"See I have to..."

"Yes, si."

"No, I'm not saying si like you say si, I'm saying see like I say see. Like listen, see?"

"Si, canceled."

And he walked away.

"Wrong line."

"I don't understand, this is the fifth line I've waited in."

"You have to go out this door then to your left…"

"No please don't make me go out that door. I've been out that door three times already. That's the exit of the airport. There are no planes out that door. Do you understand? No planes. Just sidewalk. I need to be inside of the airport to get on an airplane."

****

When I finally landed in Cusco I instantly had a headache. I'm not sure if it was from the altitude (Cusco sits at 11,000 feet above sea level) or the fact that I had met Celeste, the first member of the tour group that I would be with over the next week.

"Hi I'm Celeste? I'm from California?" Celeste said to me in that annoying California accent where you're never quite sure if they're making a statement or asking a question. She had long hair on most of her head, but the left side was shaved bald. She wore hiking pants, expensive hiking shoes, and a T-shirt that said "not my president" with a picture of Donald Trump's face with an X through it. She actually may have been good looking if she wasn't trying so hard not to be.

"Did you know that Cusco was the capital of the Incan Empire?"

"I do."

"They were so in tune with nature, so peaceful."

"Well, there was the whole human sacrifice thing."

"But then of course the white people showed up from Spain. God, I just hate white people."

"We're white."

"Well, yeah, but we're not like white-white. You know what I mean?"

"Um…"

"White's like an idea, like a power structure. It's a way to keep people down. I don't identify as white. I'm sure you don't either."

"Ah..."

"We're travelers you and I. We both receive and radiate energy as we blend with the world. Americans are consumers, they throw around their money and think they own the world. They're tourists, yuk."

Her boyfriend, Abe, a Jewish guy from Maine, rode with us from the airport too. It appeared to me that he was not allowed to speak.

"Lovely hikers! Welcome to Peru." As the car dropped us off at the hostel we were greeted by Rosel, our local tour guide for the week. He was short, fit, obviously Inca, somewhere in his late 30s I would guess. I liked him right away.

"Your head is a little opposite Mister?"

"Yeah, I've had a bit of a headache since I've landed."

"Let me get to you some coca tea, very good." He went off to the reception area. I sat down. The car ride had definitely made the headache worse.

"You notice how they don't criminalize things down here? Coca tea contains real cocaine, but nobody here cares." Celeste sat with me and rubbed the back of my head like we had known each other for ten years. I found it insanely annoying. "In the States it's a way to keep the minority populations down. You ever thought about that?"

"I don't know."

"Aye, aye mates!" A hand slapped me on the back. "I'm Rory, this is me mate Liam. From the UK, isn't that right Liam? And who are you love?"

Celeste introduced herself. If I had called her love she would have been insulted, but since it was in a British accent, I guess all was good.

Three girls from Alabama joined us next. They were in their twenties, recent college grads, all with the same haircuts and conservative dress. They told me their names and I instantly forgot all three of them.

"Ok my friends. A group of our brothers and sisters met here much earlier this morning, so I think you will not see them until our dinner tonight." Rosel told us as he handed me a coca tea. "You group may explore our beautiful village of Cusco. Before you go out please to allow me to tell you a little bit about Cusco."

I sipped my tea.

"Today my friends you will be to seeing the oldest city in all of the Americas. For over three thousand year this city is of constant peoples. This means that the people lived here in Cusco one thousand years before the coming of the Christ, never to abandon the city.

At around 1200 AD we have the beginning of the Inca people, my people. I think maybe this is why you are coming to Peru and Manchu Picchu to learn about this things, yes?"

We nodded.

"The Incas are building what we now know as the modern Cusco city. What even now we do not know is how they are building it. You will see many boulders of tremendouses sizes, and the most experts of craftmanships. It is unknown how the large stones were gathered and transported to the site, or how they manage to build with much technique so far advanced for their time.

Do you know my friends that the puma is sacred animal of my peoples? What is of much interest to you may be that the entire city of Cusco is laid out in the shape to make a puma. It is truth my friends. The fortress of Saksaywaman is the head, the plaza of Huacaypata the middle, and Tullumayo river is making the tail. So you see the entire city is a piece of art."

Celeste gasped and covered her heart with her hands.

"Next, in the 1500 we have the arrival of who my friends?"

"Spanish."

"Yes, it is the coming of how the Spanish came to be here. And there was much war for many years. The Inca peoples fight for many long times, but in the end it is the Spanish. So in 1572 the last Inca emperor, Tuqaq Amaru, was defeat and executed in the main square of the city.

Then the Spanish did many destructions and much art and treasures are lost, but still the city is survive.

Even though the Spanish have controls now, the Inca people lead many revolutions. Finally, in 1821 the country of Peru receives its independence from Spain.

In 1933 Cusco is declare the archaeological capital of South America and in 1978 it is declare a cultural heritage of the world.

So what about what you will be seeing today, yes? I think you will walk to Plaza de Armas. This is the main city square and it is the area that many year ago was called as Haukaypata, meaning the great square of the Inca. So you can see that it is many year of history.

Please to enjoy the many markets, good Peruvian food, drinks, and excitement that you will see in the plaza. But also to notice both the magnificent Cusco Cathedral and the Church La Compania de Jesus. When you are looking to them please be sure to notice the foundation. Many great buildings in the city are build on top of foundations that used to be original Inca walls.

So I think there is much history for you to see, many exciting things for you in town, and a chance to get to know you brother and sister who you will be hike with this coming week. Ok my friends, vamonos!"

People wandered off to use the bathrooms or grab something out of their rooms. Rosel took my tea cup, refilled it with fresh coca tea, and sat it down in front of me.

"My friend, how is you head?"

"I'll be ok."

"Yes, but it is still opposite?"

"Yeah, it hurts."

"It is very normal here. High altitudes. Every group of sixteen, maybe I have five or so peoples that are hurt."

"I'll get over it."

"You know about coca tea?"

"Not really."

"The Inca peoples use the coca leaves very much. Today you will drink coca tea, I think maybe it will help with you head. Later, on the trail, we will all put some coca leaf into our mouth and let the coca juices give us energies. It is very good to help make you strong for climbing and not so sick of the altitude."

Later I looked up coca tea. The coca leaf, from which cocaine is made, has been both chewed and brewed in Peru since the time of the Incas. Although there does not seem to be any medical research on the subject, they all swear that it both relieves altitude sickness and gives you the strength that you need for long-distance hiking. A line of cocaine reportedly contains between 20 and 30 mg of coca alkaloids, while coca tea in comparison contains around 4 mg. So although it is far milder than sucking white powder through your nose in a disco bathroom, chewing coca leaves, or having some coca tea, certainly could make you both feel stronger and help you ignore a headache.

****

The nine of us made our way to the busy Plaza de Armas. To get there we followed the map, only a kilometer or two from our hotel, through the streets of Cusco. They were obviously not built with cars in mind. The sides of the streets were all stone walls, with no breaks whatsoever save for doors that were about four feet tall so you could step down into mini marts, hostels, and restaurants. The stone roads were just wide enough for one car to pass, provided that we all squeezed ourselves onto the "sidewalk," which averaged only about one foot wide. It was just enough room to walk, but unfortunately all the sidewalks were two ways, so either you would have to plaster yourself against the stone wall so another walker could pass you, or you would have to gage that you had ten full seconds before the next speeding car would pass, quickly jump off the sidewalk, jog past the oncoming walker, and jump back on the sidewalk to avoid being smushed like a bug. I found it a bit overwhelming, but somehow stray dogs all seemed to understand the system perfectly.

The square was truly beautiful. Two enormous churches dominated it with a fountain of a golden Inca looking towards the mountains sitting in the middle. People were everywhere. A parade of traditionally clothed Incas walked by us.

"Should we eat?"

"Sure, what do you all want?"

"Oy! They've a McDonalds here! I could go for Big Mac. What do you say Liam?"

"Yeah mate."

"We are not eating at McDonalds!" Celeste jumped in.

For the first time I had totally agreed with Celeste, I did not come to Peru so I could eat at a McDonalds! It should be noted however that later in the afternoon, when she didn't think anyone was looking, I saw her sneak into Starbucks.

We ended up at a small Peruvian restaurant. I had Alpaca with onions, potatoes, veggies, and a scoop of white rice that I could have skipped. It was good, although I don't know if I could tell you it tasted any different than a chunk of beef stew.

The Plaza de Armas is flanked by two magnificent churches, Cathedral Basilica and Church la Compania de Jesus. We went inside Basilica.

"Wow, so beautiful," one of the girls from Alabama said. "You can really feel God here."

"I don't feel God anywhere," Abe told her. The first time I had actually heard his voice.

"You don't believe in Jesus?" she asked, genuinely puzzled.

"Nope."

"How can you not believe in Jesus?"

He thought about this for a minute. "You know how you don't believe in Zeus, Ra, Odin, Budda, or Iris? That's how."

"Yeah, but those are false gods. I'm talking about Jesus."

"It's just all so beautiful," the second girl from Alabama said.

Construction on the Cathedral began around 1550 and was

completed in 1654. God or no God, it was quite a piece of archi-
tecture. Huge pillars held up golden-domed ceilings. The floor
was made of...

"I feel the opposite of God here." We all looked at Abe. "I
see a hundred years of slave labor. I see a Catholic Church built on
top of a sacred Inca site in an attempt to wipe their history off the
Earth. And I see all the gold and jewels of the empire brought here
as decoration instead of feeding and caring for the people." He
turned to exit.

"I'll pray for you," one of the girls said as we walked out.

"We should pray," another girl from Alabama said excitedly.
"Who wants to come pray with me?"

Two of them walked forward and kneeled. I continued to
look at all the art.

"Hey." Clint, a Texan who was roughly my age, elbowed me.
"Is that Jesus eating a rat?"

I looked up at a giant painting of what, in all other ways,
appeared to be The Last Supper. Jesus and his disciples sat around
eating what was, without any doubt, a roasted rodent.

"Um." I hesitated. "I think it's a guinea pig." I had read that
they ate guinea pigs down here.

"What in the hell..." Clint stopped himself and looked
around, pausing long enough to make sure that he did not get
struck by lightning for saying hell in a church. "What in the heck
is Christ doing eating a Go... a gosh darn guinea pig?"

"Um." I had no idea. There it was though, a full guinea
pig. Claws, tail, even the head, hanging out as the main course for
Christ at the last supper. It also didn't seem to be nearly enough
food for all of them, one little guinea pig. I wondered if the disciples had a pecking order?

"Who are you again?"

"Andrew."

"Andrew? Have you been here the whole time? Anyone
know this guy?"

"I'm Peter's brother."

"That's my brother."

"And he's a disciple too?"

"Yeah."

"Fine, as long as Peter vouches for you. You can have the head."

As we walked through the square, we were endlessly approached to buy trinkets, clothes, trips, or go for a massage. Girls literally pulled on my hands while saying "Massage, massage." It didn't sound all that bad.

"Cuantos?" Celeste asked the massage girl. Then she turned to me. "That means how much does it cost."

"I know what it means."

"Viente." The girl smiled.

"Viente means..."

"Twenty." Celeste looked annoyed that I didn't allow her to teach me the basics of Spanish. "Twenty Sols."

"So like, how much is that in US dollars? Does anyone know the conversion rate?

"3.2 Dollars per Sol. So, twenty Sol is about $6.25"

"I don't think that's right?" Making a statement that she thought my math was wrong, yet still putting a question mark at the end in order to apologize for her statement.

"It is."

"You didn't use a calculator." She looked at me, then turned to the massage girl, "Cuantos en Ustedes Unidos dollars?"

"No se."

"Is that right Joel?" Rory looked shocked. "Six of your American dollars for a massage? Is she having a laugh mate?"

"No, I think she's serious."

"Well bloody hell, I'm in for an hour. What do you say boys?"

The three girls from Alabama were still busy praying, but the rest of the group was down. We had nothing else to do all day, and six dollars for an hour massage was practically free.

"Ok," I told the girl. "You have room for six people? We have five guys and one girl, good?"

"Si."

"Let's go."

"In Spanish..." Celeste told me, "...let's go is..."

"Vamonos. I know how to say let's go in Spanish."

"Then why didn't you?"

"Because she speaks English. I just held an entire conversation with her in English, why would I say one phrase in Spanish?"

The girl led the six of us through an alley with a market selling llama wool sweaters, hats, mittens, scarfs, and any other knickknack you could think of.

"I love it." Celeste put her arms up and did a full three-sixty to take in the energy of the market. "It's all so genuine."

Looked like a bunch of gringo nonsense to me. I didn't see any of the locals wearing sweaters with pictures of llamas on them. They all had on jeans and T-shirts.

The girl led us up some narrow stairs to a small back room. Half of our group was out of breath just from walking around in this thin air.

"The room." The girl showed us to a room with eight massage beds, all about one foot apart. Other girls came in and they pulled thin curtains between each bed.

"You put you clothe in basket," my girl said, then left. I took off everything except my boxers and laid down on the massage table.

I don't think I've ever had a massage before, at least not a real one. In college I was on a sports team and the girls all gave us massages after practice, which was great, and I've had girlfriends give me backrubs, but this was my first time on a real massage bed.

Light music came on. My girl began to work on my back. I hadn't slept much last night, maybe four hours sitting up on a plane. I started to drift away.

"This is right good and proper, isn't it?" Rory was about eighteen inches away from me, talking loudly through the curtain. "What do you say Liam?"

"She's getting right up in there mate." Liam, who was three or four tables to my right yelled back at him over the relaxing music. "She on your back then?"

"Right on the upper back. You know how me upper back is always aching. Ah, there you are love, give us a crack."

A few minutes of silence followed that, enough for me to drift again into a half sleep.

"What do you say Joel?" My eyes half opened. I looked down through the hole at my hiking pants and my girl's feet. Maybe he'll stop talking if I don't answer.

Then I heard him rip the curtain back.

I turned my head and sure enough, there was Rory, holding back the curtain between us.

"Have you still got your boxers on then?"

"Come on dude!"

"Don't want her to see your wanker?"

"Shut the curtain!"

"Oy Liam! Your man here still has his shorts on! Off with them now, come on lad!"

I sat up and pulled the curtain shut.

"Alright, alright. Steady on son."

I put my head back down. After a few minutes of silence my girl moved on to my calves. They weren't really sore, but we had lots and lots of walking ahead of us so it couldn't hurt. I had studied our itinerary and day one was rough. It was an eighteen-kilometer hike, with packs on, all in the sun. We would start at twelve-thousand feet above sea level and work our way up to fifteen-thousand feet. At fifteen-thousand feet the air is thinner, breathing becomes more…

"Rory, you having a tug?" Liam called from the other side of the room.

"What, are you?"

"I'm having a tug right now."

"Are you really mate?"

"Right good tug, this one. Don't know if I can last much longer."

"Hang in there old boy. Do it for the Queen."

"Will you two please shut…"

"Oy, Joel, what do you reckon you tip for a tug?"

"Jesus Christ."

"Well I'm having a tug, tell you that much, flipping right over I am. You going to have a tug Joel?"

****

"How much?"

"Setenta sols."

"Seventy? That's it?" I turned to Clint. "That's like twenty-two dollars." I was wearing a really nice alpaca-fur sweater. Light, soft, fit me well. I assume it would be over a hundred bucks in an American mall.

"It looks good on you dude."

It did. I had packed too light anyway, could use a sweater for the trek.

"Bien." I fished out a fifty and a twenty and handed them to the lady running the shop. I threw the sweater in my pack and moved on.

"You buying it?" Clint asked.

"Yeah, think of the value of this thing."

"Probably seventy or eighty bucks in America."

"Right, but that's not even what I mean. It's a nice sweater, right?"

"Yeah, sure, I guess."

"And unique. So people are going to comment on it."

"Probably."

"Hey Joel, where'd you get that sweater? 'Oh this? I picked this up in a market in Peru when I was hiking across the Andes on a trek to get to Machu Picchu, one of the seven wonders of the world.' How do you put a value on a sweater that can start a conversation like that?"

Clint looked at me for a second. Then he looked at the sweaters. "Tell her I'll take this blue one."

"You didn't haggle?" Celeste asked us.

"Naw."

"And you bought two?"

"Well I bought one and Clint bought one, so just let me do the math, yeah, that's two."

"You could have probably gotten them for sixty sol each, maybe even fitty."

"Doesn't matter to me. That's five bucks. I like the sweater, it fits me, it's plain grey, I'm going to own it for ten years and probably wear it twenty days a year. What do I care about five bucks? Means a lot more to her than it does to me."

"You're supposed to haggle down here. It's actually considered rude if you don't."

"What?"

"That's ok, you learned something today. That's what travelling is all about."

After that I decided it was time for me to break off from the group and wander the streets by myself for awhile.

I ducked in and out of markets, avoided the massage girls, ignored the men who quietly offered weed and cocaine, and found myself in a quiet back alley passing another American wearing an equally silly explorer hat.

"Hey!" He excitedly said to me. I obviously did not blend in as a Peruvian. "Do you know where Bagel Café is?" He looked at me then back down at his phone. "This thing says I'm here, but..."

"Sorry man, I've been walking for awhile but I haven't seen a Bagel Café." Or anything like it at all. He cussed a little then went back to mumbling to his phone.

I walked a little further. The streets were all narrow cobblestone with thick cobblestone walls on both sides. They were built in an era when automobiles were not even a part of science fiction. Nothing was flat, you either walked sharply down the hill, or you dragged yourself up the hill. Even these short walks, up small hills, were tiring me out. At the top of each hill sat a gringo searching for oxygen, so at least I wasn't the only one.

Down I went, with no real destination in mind. I saw a tiny open door, with the typical knickknacks behind it. I don't know why, but I decided to duck in. It quickly opened up to a large enclosed courtyard with various vendor booths, massage, and some sort of a small restaurant.

As soon as I entered the courtyard a beautiful, I mean really stunning, Scandinavian girl gave me a huge smile and waved. I smiled back.

"Hello," she said as I walked nearer.

"Enjoying Cusco?" I asked.

"Yes, it is all so beautiful."

"I'm heading out tomorrow, trekking to Machu Picchu."

"Yes, I am just back. You will love it."

There was an open seat at her table, so I sat. "Tell me about it."

"Where to start?" So she told me about "the beauty of walking through the clouds, the sunsets in the mountains, the lack of oxygen and the endless uphills, the amazing changes when you hike down to the rainforest..." I couldn't remember ever meeting a girl so easily.

The waitress, who was on Peruvian time, finally arrived with menus.

"Maybe just a drink then we will walk together for dinner, yes?" She smiled at me.

I didn't understand how this was happening, but I went with it. "Perfect." I said and ordered an ice tea. She did the same. "And Machu Picchu itself, did you love it?"

"Oh yes." She went on and on about Machu Picchu. The engineering, the setting of a city on the mountain top, the amazing amount of structures that were still standing allowing you to really envision what it looked like five-hundred years ago.

As she was talking, the American guy who I had run into thirty minutes ago came into the courtyard, still mumbling to his phone.

He looked at the girl I was sitting with. He looked at me. He wore the biggest *what the F?* look I've ever seen on a guy's face!

I sipped my ice tea and noticed the logo on the menu. We

were at The Bagel Café.

Sweating profusely, he lumbered over to our table. Again, he looked at her. Then he pulled out his phone, looked at it for a moment, then back at her. Utterly confused he looked at me again. Not sure what to say to me, he turned back to her.

"Astrid?"

"Yes, it is me."

She looked confused. He looked both confused and pissed. He removed his trekking hat, revealing wispy hair soaked with sweat. Again, he looked at me, unsure what to say. I sipped my ice tea. Finally, he blurted out, "Who are you?"

"I'm Joel."

"You are not Mark?" Astrid looked at me.

"Hi." I reached across the table and took her hand. "I'm Joel."

"I'm Mark!" Mark more or less yelled as I held her hand.

"You are Mark?"

"Yes, we've been talking for a week! I'm Mark!" He showed her his Tinder app on his phone.

"And you are…"

"Very glad to meet you. Another ice tea?"

"I'm Mark!" he said again louder.

"This is awkward," Astrid said. "You are very nice on the Tinder, but Joel and I have had a very pleasant conversation. I believe we will leave for dinner now, yes?"

"Absolutely."

I took her hand and we got up. Mark still stood there with a dumb look on his face.

"You don't mind picking up the check, do you Mark? Just a couple of ice teas."

****

"I thought you were going to miss the meeting dude."

Clint and I were back in our hotel room, scrambling around at quarter after 8. We were fifteen minutes late, but Celeste had already told us that we were on Peruvian time now and the meeting wouldn't start for another thirty minutes. She added in that we should quit being such Americans.

"I was with a Norwegian girl in the square," I told Clint.

"Seriously?"

"She may have been from Denmark."

"That's awesome!"

"Yeah, it was alright. We're going to meet up again in a few hours."

"Dude." He gave me some knuckles. "How did you meet her?"

"Bagel Café. I pretended to be Mark from Tinder."

"Huh?"

"It's a long story."

"Ok, I'm heading down. You ready?"

"I'm just going to use the bathroom, see you down there."

Clint left and I went into the bathroom. I sat on the toilet and did what people do when they're sitting on a toilet. When I was done I scanned the room for the toilet paper. It didn't exist.

I looked again. No paper appeared.

How can there be a toilet and no toilet paper? It didn't make any sense. And yet these were the facts of the case.

I got up, pants still around my ankles, knees wide, and did a duck walk to my backpack.

I had thought ahead to bring a small toilet paper roll, one of my better choices while packing, and put it to use. It occurred to me that I may want to stockpile a bit more prior to starting our trek.

When I was done, I zipped up and walked to the door. It was locked. I looked at it, confused. I tried the door again, locked. I wasn't locked *out* of the room; I was locked *in* the room! There was no way to unlock the door. I needed the key. Clint had the key.

I looked at the door again. I tried the door again. It was locked.

I walked back into the room and, thankfully, found a

phone. I picked it up and dialed the front desk.

"Como?"

"Yeah, I'm locked in my room."

"Yes sir, come to front desk please."

They hung up. I stood there with a phone in my hand listening to a dial tone. I called back.

"Como?"

"Room 307. I'm not locked out of the room; I'm locked in the room! In!"

"Very good room sir."

"Tu tanga llave?" I said in my rough Spanish. I thought I was asking him if he had a key to the room, but I later was told that I somehow called him a women's thong.

A few more calls to the front desk and finally I was released from my room in time for the end of our group's meeting. Clint handed me a hot mug of coca tea, which I was already really starting to like. I had to agree with Celeste: a little bit of cocaine in the mornings might be nice, seems that a mild coca tea ought to be legal in America.

"The Inca peoples build over twenty-nine thousand kilometers of roads. There are many trails which are all Inca trail. So I think maybe we will take the Salkantay pass through the mountains. This sounds nice, yes?"

We all nodded. Sure.

"This is very old Incan road and I think you will see many things and learn much about the Incan peoples. Thank you my friends, so we will see you in the mornings."

Everyone went their own way. I had spent the entire meeting locked in our room.

"Did I miss anything?" I asked Clint.

"Naw, bunch of walking. Where were you dude?"

****

"They're all upside down." Astrid rested her head on my shoulder as we looked at the stars. Around us couples walked hand in hand through the Plaza de Armas. "I think that's the Big Dipper, but all the water would pour right out."

"Did you know that over twenty five percent of the population of Cusco live in poverty?" Astrid asked me in what was really a rhetorical question.

"I did not." I went in for a kiss.

In retrospect it was a very odd set-up question for us to start making out, but hey, it worked.

CHAPTER 3: GET ON THE BUS!

In the morning my headache had doubled.

Clint, my roommate, gave me some pills that his doctor had prescribed to him for altitude sickness. "They take about twenty-four hours to get into your system," he told me.

I nodded and swallowed them down. I take very few pills; I rarely even take an aspirin. Today I was willing to just swallow pills without even asking what they were.

Breakfast was in the hotel lobby.

"None of that coca for me, proper cup of English tea in the morning. Joel, fancy a cup of tea?"

I slowly shook my head no.

"Built the British Empire on a cup of tea."

"And how'd that work out?" Clint asked from my table. He was from Texas and didn't really trust anyone who wasn't.

I looked at the meager scoop of scrambled eggs I had on my plate, the single piece of bread with jam. It wasn't much, but I couldn't eat it. I poured myself a glass of some sort of fruit and yogurt smoothie and forced myself to at least finish that and my coca tea.

"Ok hikers! It is a good morning to you all, yes?"

Everyone cheered. I felt green.

"You all sleep like baby alpaca." Rosel smiled, then he looked at me. "And what about you my friend?" How is you head this morning?"

I didn't feel like talking, so I gave him a half-hearted army salute instead. I'm sure it was a stupid-looking gesture, but I saw

Indiana Jones do it right before I left so it seemed like an Alpha move at the time.

"I think maybe you will feel better in another day, yes?"

I didn't say anything. When I am at full health, I can do anything. But when I get sick it scares the hell out of me. I'm extremely used to my body working. Working perfectly. Working better, longer, and harder than anyone else's body is capable of. When I'm slumped in a chair in Peru, watching uneaten eggs and toast with my head in my hands, doubts start to run through my mind.

I'm not going to be able to make this trek.

I'm dying.

I'm going to get left behind.

Even if I go, I'm going to have diarrhea on the side of the trail every thirty minutes.

Rosel was rambling on and on, I sat with my head in my hands, mouth open, looking down at my shoes.

I should have bought better hiking shoes. Mine were clunky, old, and had originally cost only 29.99 at Meijer, a Midwest version of Walmart. As I could only stare at the floor, I noticed that everyone else wore high-end hiking shoes from expensive sports outfitters.

"My friends, you have had a good breakfast now we will see and learn some about the Incan peoples, the land, and the histories that we will be traveling. Please to get on the bus."

****

The bus. If there is a worse place in the world to have a headache than a Peruvian bus with no air vents, no open windows, and no bathroom, being driven by a little man just inches away from cliffs that would mean sure and sudden death, well, I have no idea where that place is.

I sipped water to make me feel better. It made me have to pee.

"Let's have some music then, eh!" Rory yelled from the back.

"You wish Peruvian music?"

"We'll have a listen, isn't that right lads?"

So then it started. Take suffocating heat, bumpy dirt roads, insanely high switchbacks, and add to it Peruvian noise. I shut my eyes and leaned back to try to get some sleep. My head banged off the window.

"So today first we will stop at the llama farms and see how it is that we are making the sweaters. I think it will be very nice for you as you will get to pet the llama and also take a picture. We will be there in one hour less or minus."

Oh god.

****

"So here we have the llamas."

I felt a bit better as I sat outside in a shady spot. We were at a llama farm, sort of a petting zoo for tourists.

"The llama is very important to the Incan peoples. From then, and even to now, we are using the llama for beast of burdens, carrying things, for its fur to make clothe, and yes my friends even more meat as foods."

"No!" the three girls from Alabama all said in unison. "But they're so cute!"

"Do you know that the llama is the oldest domesticate animal in the worlds?"

"Older than the dog?"

"Yes, my friends, it is true. Even before people had the dog, they had the llama."

A later Google search on my part would not support Rosel on this statement, but what the hell did I know? And really, what is Google? How do they know? Maybe the llama really was the first domesticated animal, or maybe not. At any rate it had been a large part of the Incan and Peruvian cultures for an extremely long time.

"A llama can carry maybe about 50 kg or 100 pound of weight. It is very strong. But if you try to give too much the weight, what will the llama do? He will sit down. The llama is not shy about not liking you. What will the llama do if he does not like you my friends?"

"Sit down?"

"The llama will spit at you."

"OMG, gross!"

"But no to worry, today I believe the llama will be very happys as we are going to take some of this rich grass, one big handful each, and feed the llamas. You may make a good picture now. After we will go inside and see how it is that we are weaving the llama fur into very nice sweaters, mittens, and hats, and you will have opportunity to find some presents for you friends back home. Now, come, we feed the llamas and make a picture!"

We all grabbed a handful of lush greens and broke off on our own to feed, pet, and photograph llamas. We may have suddenly become a bunch of elementary children at a petting zoo, but we liked it.

****

"Sixty-two bottles of beer on the wall, sixty-two bottles of beer..."

The whole gang sang along as our bus bounced over potholes and zipped by hairline turns with the wheels inches from the cliff.

One of the girls from Alabama looked out her window to see the sheer hundred yard drop off that would happen if our driver drifted a few inches in the wrong direction.

"Oh heck no." She got up and moved to the other side of the bus.

"Yeah, that will save you." Clint laughed.

"Fifty-seven bottles of beer!"

"You look like you might throw up," Clint told me. I halfway shut my eyes as I gave him a thumbs-up sign.

****

"So my friends. Soon we will hike to the top, it is maybe

one hundred and fifty stairs only, and from there we will have some nice view and picture. But first we are learning a little bit more about how it is that the Incas are farming."

We were at an archeological site. I sat at the back of the group and listened as much as I could. The mountain had been flattened into fifty or so large terraces. The flat land allowed them to grow five times more food than they could on a slanted mountain; they also were able to equip the terraces with an irrigation system.

"Ok, vamanos!"

Rosel led the group; they all rose to go up the mountain with him. I did not. This wasn't me. I'm not the guy at the bottom of the hill. But I was.

Rory was the last member of the line that was slowly leaving me.

"Hey Rory." They walked on. "Rory!"

He turned. "Alright then son?"

"Let Rosel know I'm staying down here." Our hike didn't begin until tomorrow. This was the pregame, the warmup, it didn't matter. There was no reason for me to make myself sicker. Tomorrow would be Go Day, like it or not, but I didn't need to push it today.

"What, you're staying here then?"

"Yeah."

"Bullocks to all that, I'll stay with you."

"You don't have…"

"I want to mate. Those stairs are a right pain, aren't they? Oy! Liam! Let your man Rosel know that Joel and me are heading out. We're going to have a pint at the bottom."

"Aye aye." Liam turned and climbed after the rest of the group.

"I'm not having a pint."

"One of your American coffees then, eh? Come on son, put your left foot forward, your right one will follow, they call it walking."

"You like birds then mate?"

"Yeah, sure." I sipped my coffee. Rory and I sat at the bottom of the ruin in a tiny town set up only for the day tourists. There was a coffee place, a few places with food, a pub, and of course a market selling gringo nonsense. "I don't really know much about them."

"About what?"

"Birds."

"What's to know? A peach is a peach if ya know what I mean!" He pointed at the ass of a girl in leggings.

"Ah, *birds*. Well you're not wrong about that."

"Aye aye."

He really wasn't wrong. This place was a virtual world buffet. Rory and I sipped our coffees and watched girls from America, Ireland, Brazil, Scandinavia, Israel, local Peru girls, every sort of Asian... They all had one thing in common: every one of them worked out and believed themselves fit enough to undertake a five-day mountain trek. Rosel was wrong, the good views were down here.

"Look at this bender." Rory pointed to what looked like a Spanish couple. "Can you believe she is with him? Bloody tosser he is." If you sat at our table you would soon learn that there wasn't a single guy in the village that was good enough for any one of the girls, except for the two of us of course.

****

"Take one down, pass it around, eighty-seven bottles of beer on the wall! Eighty-seven bottles of beer on the wall, eighty-seven bottles of beer..."

The air and the coffee had cleared my head a bit, and I had found a toilet in town, not always an easy thing to do I was learning.

"Media sol." The old women had held out her hand to me before I would be allowed into the toilet. Half a sol, that's about fifteen cents, I believe. I dug around and pulled out a handful of change.

"Um..."

She reached into my hand and pulled out a coin. I assume it was the right one, but who knows?

She handed me two squares of toilet paper.

I stepped forward, but a blind man stepped in front of me and went into the toilet. I made a face, but that's all I did, all I could do. So I stood there, waiting for a blind man to finish peeing all over the place.

Now I was back on the bus. The air, coffee, water, and toilet had all helped.

"...pass it around, eight-three bottles of beer on the wall!" The headache was coming back, and it was bringing friends.

An hour later I again sat at the bottom of another ruin. Rosel had sent the group on a self-guided tour, now he shared a bit of shade and cool grass with me.

"Tomorrow, it is very difficult."

"Yep, well, it is what it is."

"I think it is only eighteen kilometers, but we will climb from maybe twelve thousand feet to over fifteen-thousand feet."

"I'll be fine."

"I will have oxygen with me. Also will Raul, our other guide of who you will be meeting tomorrow."

"Won't need oxygen."

"There is not so much an ambulance, but we have a mule, just in case a hiker cannot continue then we can put on the mule."

"Don't need a mule."

"It is not to be afraid; the mule is very good footing and easy to ride."

"I can ride anything with four legs, and I'm not afraid, I'm an American. But I won't be riding a damned mule because I'm going to be hiking."

"Also there is the porters. They can carry you bag."

"I carry my own bag. Nobody carries my bag."

"I think maybe it is not so smart with you level of altitude sickness."

"You have kids?" I asked him in an effort to change the subject.

"Yes, two kids. In Lima. But my wife, she kick me out. I think it is not so easy with my job."

"See them often?"

"When I can. I lead a hike almost every week, but sometimes on the weekend I am able to go to Lima."

"That's good. Be the best dad that you can, that's all you can do."

"Yes. It is true. You are father?"

I showed him a picture of my kids and he shook my hand.

"And you're still a young man," I told him. "You can always get married again, even have more kids if you want."

"Maybe I am getting old? Too old for always hike."

"Naw. You're what, thirty-five years old?"

"Thank you, my friend. But on this hike I will have my birthday and on which I will have forty-one years of age."

"Well, that's not old."

"No, but maybe it is for always hiking and tours. But what else can I do? I don't know." We sat for a few moments. He opened a water bottle.

****

In the evening we rolled into our accommodations for the night. At the foot of the Salcantay mountain sat a dozen or so cabanas, all with glass walls and ceilings. The stars were out, the night air was crisp, and I was sharing an incredibly romantic cabana with a Texan named Clint.

"Hey Joel check it out!" He flipped all the lights off and pointed over to the glass cabana with the three Alabama girls. Their lights were on and they were changing clothes for the night. Clint stood there, in the dark, leering at them like a like a pathetic 1950s peeping Tom. I was disgusted with him, and as soon as I was done watching the girls change, I would let him know.

The food was of a much higher quality than I had antici-pated. Bowls of homemade soups, garlic bread, roasted vege-tables, stuffed chicken, local side dishes, all prepared fresh by our team of porters.

I tried to figure out what they ate, and when. I am not at all certain, but I think that they may have gotten the leftovers. That made me feel bad, but I have to be honest, at the moment I did not care. My head pounded. My stomach turned over. My bowels warned me that I would likely have diarrhea on the side of the trail multiple times tomorrow. The truth is when a person feels like that, or at least when I do, the only thing I care about is myself. It is easy to be charitable when you are rich, easy to care about others when you are healthy. For me, when I'm sick, I just want to survive.

"I'm not going to make this trek," I thought to myself. I had finished my bowl of soup. That actually tasted good and went down really well. But now it was time for solid food.

"Yes you are," a voice in my mind shot back.

"I'm not. I can't make it."

"You can and you will. Now stop your whimpering!"

I took the minimum amount of solid food to make up one small plate, then I started picking at it slowly.

Rosel noticed me. "Your body is weak?"

"My body is the exact opposite of weak."

"But maybe you feel not so comfortable in the mountain? It is very high up."

"What time are we leaving tomorrow?"

"I think maybe six in the a.m. We will have wake-up ser-vice at five."

I looked at my phone, it was 11 p.m. Great. I could have slept for nine or ten hours. We had the toughest hike that the vast majority of us have ever been on coming up tomorrow, and they were giving us just six hours of sleep.

I pushed my plate away and got up. I could feel Rosel look-ing at me as I made my way to bed.

The glass cabana was amazing. There was zero light interference in the mountains. Our walls and ceiling were a perfect dome of glass panels: moonlight poured into the room and made visibility possible without having to use our headtorches. It was one of the nicest settings I've ever been in.

I enjoyed it for roughly seventeen seconds before rolling over for a much-needed sleep.

CHAPTER 4: A SLAVE IN EYGPT

Six hours later there was a knock on our door.

"Lovely hikers."

Rosel knocked again. Clint stumbled out of his bed and opened it.

"Good morning my friends, I hope you sleep like baby alpaca!"

Clint and I both mumbled something without really making any effort at speaking in any language.

"Yes. I think it will be a very hard day of much hiking, but also very rewarding for you when you are on the top of the mountain tonight. Here is some room service of coca tea and we will be meeting you in the main building for breakfast in thirty minutes. Please have you pack all ready, yes?"

Clint handed me a hot metal mug of coca tea as he mumbled something else and closed the door.

"Want another one of those altitude sickness pills?"

"Yeah." He handed me one and I washed it down with my morning ration of liquid cocaine. "If you have enough, I'll just take one every morning and every night."

"I have plenty. Doc gave me a month supply even though I'm only in Peru for a week."

We got to the business of packing up our stuff. Roughly half would go ahead with the mules, while we would carry whatever we thought we might actually need during the day. I had packed so little to begin with, only a school-sized backpack, that I just sent my sleeping bag and a few other minor things ahead.

The one thing I made sure to bring was my spare toilet paper. I was scared to death that I was going to need it many times on the trail today, but much more scared that I would need it and not have it!

The food was truly amazing. When I had signed up for this tour, which was relatively inexpensive, they had promised three meals a day. I had expected breakfast to be a pile of granola bars next to a pile of bananas. If I was lucky, I would find oatmeal, and hopefully there would also be coffee. The reality was a variety of hot drinks, and a steaming bowl of local porridge, as soon as we sat down in the mornings. Roughly ten minutes later the porters would load the table up with meats, cheeses, breads, a medley of local fruits, and eggs.

I eyed it all, and knew that I could not eat. I forced myself to finish my warm bowl of quinoa porridge. It tasted really good, put a little bit of food in me, and started off the day with a bit of water in me as well. Others reached for their second helping of everything. I eyed the rest of the food, but just couldn't touch it.

If I wanted to, I could use my headache to take my pulse, every beat of my heart throbbed in my head.

It turns out that girls do poop. The male and female bathrooms were separated by a thin wall that started about six inches above the floor, and ended a couple feet shy of the ceiling. As I had my morning diarrhea I hoped that nobody on the other side was listening in too closely.

I finished up, wiped thoroughly, while still being careful to conserve much needed paper, and exited to wash my hands in the sink. Then I quickly turned, doubled over, and vomited.

Outside everyone was shouldering their packs, tightening their shoes, stretching their quads.

"Mister Joel!" Rosel caught up with me. "How is you head feeling this morning?"

"Perfect."

"Yes? And you stomach? It is no opposite?"

"My stomach feels great."

"So no more sickness of altitude?"

"No more."

"Very good my friend. But you will tell if any signs is coming back?"

"Of course."

He smiled and patted me on the back.

Men in the NBA take to the courts with fevers of 102 degrees, burning up from the flu, and put up fifty points that night before collapsing in the locker room. Today was my game day. All I had to do was put on a pack and climb a mountain into thin air.

****

From the minute Rosel said "vamanos" our group instantly became spread out. Five of our group were trail runners, two married couples in their late thirties or early forties, and a twenty-three-year-old girl who had done multiple mountain marathons. This was their thing, high-altitude hiking up hills, and running down the declines. They wanted to go fast, fast, fast.

I fell in with Ed, a sixty-four-year-old army veteran who, at least to the naked eye, had not done a day of PT since he was honorably discharged over twenty years ago.

"Had three kids," he was telling me. "The youngest just turned forty. When you're just a dumb grunt you start early. Divorced of course, don't know anyone who isn't, that's par for the course too. Got a girlfriend now. Nice girl, from the Philippines. Kids don't like her, but that's no surprise."

He stopped talking and stood still for a minute to catch his breath. We were roughly a quarter mile from the cabanas and still on flat ground. Rosel told us that we would be hiking eighteen kilometers today, but I don't think the hike had even started yet. It appeared to be roughly a mile walk until we exited the last of the little settlements set up for the hikers that come through here daily. Then, after a mile of walking, we would *begin* the hike.

Ed caught his breath and we moved on. The trail runners

were far ahead but, luckily, we had a few serious photographers in the group as well. They were a good hundred yards behind us, so I wasn't dragging and being left by the group just yet. Of course, the hike hadn't even started yet.

"Tried to get her to come on this trip with me," he continued, struggling for air again. "But you know the Philippines..."

"I was actually just there a few months ago."

"Well it's hot there."

"Yep."

"Hot as all hell."

"Yep."

"She read about the cold temperatures up in the mountains and that was that, I was told to book a trip for one."

I of course read just about nothing prior to flying to Peru. As far as cold temperatures were concerned, I was woefully unprepared. I had one base layer, a llama sweater that I had not bargained for, and one light pull-over from REI. I also did not pack any rain gear, and despite it saying "very important" on the packing list we had received from the tour, I did not bring a headtorch. They were about fifty dollars at REI and I just said screw it.

Ed stopped again to catch his breath and I watched him struggle.

At sea level, where the vast majority of us live, the atmosphere is twenty-one percent oxygen. In areas that we Americans consider high altitude, for example parts of Colorado or New Mexico, they are roughly eight-thousand feet up. There, oxygen makes up only fifteen to sixteen percent of the atmosphere. A lot of people have problems with that while visiting Colorado. Here, at the base of Salkantay, we were at twelve-thousand feet. The air was only thirteen percent oxygen. Mathematically that means that there was only sixty-two percent as much oxygen in the air here as there was at home. In other words, it took three full breaths to get the amount of oxygen that you would normally get in two breaths.

Thus far, the hike was still flat. Soon we would be heading up, up, and up. It was hard work to climb up a mountain, and every step we took would bring us into slightly thinner air. By the end of the day we would be at fifteen-thousand feet above sea level, where there is only half of the amount of oxygen that we have become used to our entire lives. Half the oxygen.

Abe, a full-time unemployed social justice warrior from Maine, caught up with us.

"Magnificent, isn't it." He pointed up to the peak of Salkantay. It was. It also just looked high as hell.

Abe glanced at Ed, who had just now caught his breath, nodded to me, and moved on. "You train at all for the hike man?"

"Twenty years of humping gear in the infantry. If that isn't training, then I don't know what is boy."

Yes, I thought to myself, but that was twenty years ago.

****

Thirty minutes after we left breakfast we arrived at the base of the mountain. It was time to really start our day's hike.

"Ok my friends. Now we will be beginning our hike to Humantay lake. It will take maybe one and a half hours to get to the lake, and I think maybe it is very steep but it will be very rewarding and fresh when we arrive. So you will see on you hike both the Salkantay mountain and Hamantay peak that is feeding the glacier water into this beautiful crystal-clear waters. When we are there we can relax, have a snack, go to a swim, and maybe as a group we will give thanks to Pachamama which is how we are calling the Mother Earth."

And now we started going up.

I pushed aside my insane altitude sickness, leaned on my hiking poles, and started the trek to drag my ass up to Humantay lake. It was two miles of steep climbing. We had to go from twelve thousand to fifteen thousand feet today, a total gain of three thousand feet. By the time we reached the lake we will have ascended twelve hundred feet. That's a good start, I told myself. Then we're have a nice long rest at the lake.

I saw Rory ahead of me and remembered his words from

yesterday: "Come on son, put your left foot forward, your right foot will follow. They call it walking." Up I walked.

I walked for fifty yards. Then I stopped. My breath was gone. My heartrate felt like it was up around a hundred and fifty. I leaned heavy on my poles and caught my breath.

I looked ahead. Others were struggling, even the trail runners. Down below half of our group stood huffing and puffing.

Ok, I said in between breaths as I started to recover. *You see that clump of bushes about twenty-five yards ahead? You can make it there.*

I passed the clump of bushes and moved on up to the next one, then stopped again for air.

Drink some water. I thought to myself. The more you drink the more hydrated you are and the less your pack weighs.

I walked again, setting my sights on the next landmark then stopping again.

Halfway up I again doubled over on my poles and searched for air.

Rosel, who was wearing a pack twice as heavy as any of ours, gently walked right by me. He was playing the flute.

Let me say this again. As he walked up the hill, carrying a heavy pack, at thirteen thousand feet, while I gasped for air, this obnoxious little bugger was playing the flute.

Rosel was Inca. The Incans had lived at extreme altitude for centuries, and perhaps longer.

Incans have been able to adapt to their high-altitude living through successful acclimatization, which is characterized by increasing oxygen supply to the blood tissues. For the native Inca living in the Andean highlands, this was achieved through the development of a larger lung capacity, and an increase in red blood cell counts. Compared to other humans, the Incans have slower heart rates, almost one-third larger lung capacity, about two liters more blood volume, and double the amount of hemoglobin, which transfers oxygen from the lungs to the rest of the body. The result is the ability to play a flute while trekking uphill.

The rest of us struggled for the next hour.

"Ah, my nuts!" I heard Clint yell as he went balls deep into the frozen glacier water. I was hidden, doubled over behind a boulder, spitting up what little water I had taken in and dry heaving.

I wiped my mouth, took a very small drink, and returned to the group, finding a rock to sit on. I don't think anyone had noticed me vomiting, but Rory saw me sitting while the other young men were all getting ready to swim.

"Come on, man up now son," Rory mocked as he stripped down revealing a body that could easily win "Whitest Man of the Year" award anywhere off of his little island. He then stepped into the water himself. "Bloody hell!" He stepped back out.

"Cold then is it?" Liam asked as he revealed a never-ending display of tattoos.

"I told you so!" Clint said as he dunked himself.

"Taters in the mould mate!"

"Is it really, that bad?"

"Proper!"

I kept my clothes on. Humantay Lake was gorgeous, and on any other day I would have gone for a swim, but I was ill enough without compounding the day's problems by getting "taters in the mould" cold, whatever the hell that was.

I was missing an experience, I knew, but it just wasn't the day for it.

I pulled a banana and a pack of saltine crackers out of my pack. While the others, about half the group, swam, I forced myself to eat just a little and to finish about a liter of water.

"How is it?" I asked Clint as he climbed out.

"Cold, man. Takes your breath away."

The lake was a basin at the bottom of the snowcapped Humantay and Salkantay peaks. The water was crystal blue; it looked like an ad for a company that sells bottled water.

Clint, like he was reading my mind, took it all in and said, "Man, this place is like a screen saver."

"Condor!" Abe yelled and I quickly turned my head.

We all spun around. I got to see the great bird, just for a second, maybe two, float over our heads and disappear on the other side of the hill. We waited for him to reappear, but he did not.

"Wow, very nice my friends. Did you all have a look? This was the condor of Peru, largest bird in the world. Most groups are not experiencing this wonder. The condor will live very high up, normal building of its nest at fifteen, even sixteen-thousand feet."

"How high are we now?"

"Thirteen-thousand-and-seven-hundred foot is the elevation of Humantay lake."

Thirteen-thousand, seven-hundred! We had already climbed seventeen-hundred feet. We had only thirteen-hundred more feet to ascend today. We were more than halfway up. I could make this!

"This names of condor is from the Quechua language, my language. Quechua is the language of my peoples, the Incan peoples. So sometimes I am speaking with you in English, sometimes in Spanish, then with the porters and guides I will be speaking mostly in the Quechua. Some of you are speaking Spanish, yes?"

I understood some Spanish, and spoke much less. A few others on our tour actually spoke Spanish.

"Sometime you will hear me speaking to other guides and you will not understand what it is we are talking."

"I'm fluent." Abe, who had lived all of his thirty-seven years in a college bubble, told him, "and I have no idea what you're saying."

"This is because not only does Peru Spanish have its own accent that is much different from Mexico, but also because here, in my home of the Andes, we speak maybe half in Spanish and half the words is Quechua, mixing them together very fast.

So the condor is the word from the Quechua language. How long is it living? Well some adult condor can live for more than fifty years and in captivity, in the zoo, some are report to have lived for even seventy year.

In Peru the condor is very important as it is our national bird, but more so it is of great importance to the Incan peoples. We can find the condor in Incan art from as old as two-thousand and five-hundred years before the Christ.

We are also using the condor as our representative to display the willingness of the Inca people to continue to resist and fight the Spanish invaders. We will have what is known as the Yawar Festival in which the condor is tie to the back of a bull. Why a bull? A bull is Spanish while a condor is Inca. So the condor is tie to the back of the bull. The bull try to get it off, but it cannot. Slowly the condor will dig with its claws, how do you say?"

"Talons."

"Yes, talons, it will dig with its talons until the bull is die."

"I can't." Celeste put up her hand to indicate that she simply could not hear any more, as if her hand would stop sound from coming through it.

"Even today the condor is seen by the Inca peoples as not only a sign of power and health, but also as a representative of the living sun god and the ruler of the upper world.

Every day the condor soars above us in its search for feeding. It may travel as a loop of as much as two-hundred kilometers in only one day. So, who knows, maybe this condor has already even see the Machu Picchu today.

Let us put back on our packs and with the strength and health that the condor has blessed upon us we will resume our hiking."

We put our gear on and picked up our hiking poles.

Ed, a sweaty mess, came huffing and puffing around the corner. "Is this the lake?"

****

We walked the kilometer from the lake back to the main trail. Once there I expected to turn left and continue our ascent. But Rosel turned right, momentarily descending down the very hill we had just climbed.

Walking down the hill was certainly much easier on the lungs, but I couldn't help but realize that every step I took was giving up one step of hard-fought ground. We continued down for about five minutes.

How far down would we go before we joined another trail and started going up again? We must have lost a few hundred feet already!

"How far down are we going?" I asked Clint.

"I have no idea."

Down we went.

Then we went further down.

I wanted to ask Rosel how far down are we going! We were perhaps twenty-five percent of the way down already. That was ground that we were going to have to make up for later today! Would we join the trail going up soon? But I could not ask Rosel, he was too far ahead and moving down at too rapid of a pace. The five trail runners jogged at his heels.

The answer was: we went all the way down. One-hundred percent of the way down. Every damned foot that we had worked and sweated for was gone.

Thirty minutes after we had left the lake, we gathered up at the bottom of the hill.

"Ok my friends, now that we have seen the lake, we will now be beginning our trek to Machu Picchu, yes!"

The group cheered. My head pounded. It was ten a.m. now, the sun was fully out, not a bit of shade to be found.

"So we are around maybe twelve-thousand feet. By lunch we will be around fourteen thousand, maybe fourteen thousand and five hundred. Then, after we have a lovely meal, we will continue to climb for maybe two more hour. This will bring us to fifteen thousand-feets. It is very important that we do little by little, yes, as the air is no so strong. If we try to go very fast it is why some people are naming today The Gringo Killer."

I took another sip of water. My stomach held down the banana and the crackers, I didn't think I was going to vomit again.

"So if anyone is feeling opposite we have with us two mules

today for riding."

Won't be riding a mule, I said to myself as my head throbbed.

"After we have reached the peaks, then it is maybe three more hour of nice hiking, flat, maybe even a little downhills, through the clouds. Then we will have reached the campsite.

So I think it is all about today my friends. If we can make it to the top of the mountains then the hiking only get easier and easier. But for today, maybe four or five hours more, it is very steep, with many rock, and lots of sun. Ok please to have a sip of water then we will begin."

The trail racers zipped ahead. The guys were both around six-feet tall and weighed maybe 150lbs each, one-hundred percent muscle and most of it in their legs. The women were around 5'7" and couldn't have been more than 125 lbs. Beth, the college girl who came with them, had endless energy. She bounded up as easily as a porter. I normally don't have trouble keeping up with anyone on a hike, but that wasn't going to happen today.

"I think a little by little is the way to go." I heard Rosel in my head. I set my sights on a large boulder about twenty-five yards in front of me and walked to it. Then I rested. Then I did it again.

Behind me the group fanned out. Everyone dug hard into their trekking poles, pulled themselves up a few more rocky steps, then rested.

I turned my mind off, put what was left of my body on autopilot, and hiked.

****

"You are doing good my friend?" I heard Rosel asking me without even noticing that I was passing him. He was sitting on a big rock, waiting for everyone to pass, checking on us.

"Yeah." I managed to get out the one syllable word before doubling over, leaning on my hiking poles, and gasping for oxygen. In reality I was not feeling good. I felt like a slave in ancient Egypt being forced to build a pyramid.

Pick this rock up, carry it over to the pyramid, then run on back and get the next rock. Repeat that all day, every day, seven days a week until you die. Pyramid isn't finished yet? No problem, have a son, we'll put him to work too.

"I think maybe you would like to ride a mule?"

"Don't....." gasp "need" gasp "a" two gasps "god damn mule."

I sat with Rosel for five minutes.

Abe showed up and half sat half fell onto the rocks next to us. He pulled out his water bottle but had to wait a full minute to catch his breath before he could drink. For the past two days I had listened to his nonstop badmouthing of America (it was always a rich white American male like Abe who badmouthed America). Our criminal justice system is out to get people of color, trans people are literally dying and we don't care, we're not providing adequate medical care for undocumented citizens. The nonstop unsolicited opinions grew quite tiresome when all I wanted to do was look at the stars.

But there were no opinions right now, just a skinny bearded man with wispy hair gasping for air.

Ed passed us, riding on top of a mule lead by a porter. He took a drink from his water bottle. "Goddamn hot out here," and rode off.

It was. It was also time for me to move on. I wanted to go before Abe caught his breath and told me about the latest thing that Trump had done.

I put my pack on and pulled myself to my feet.

"Ok my friend, I will stay here until the last hiker then I will pass you."

"Yep, I'm sure you will."

"You have only maybe ten kilometers more, more or minus, until the top."

"Great."

Again I put one foot in front of the other and just kept walking. There were other tours on the mountain and I gently passed them.

"Avalanche!"

I heard it at the same time that the women yelled the word and pointed to Salkantay mountain about a kilometer away.

I was a split second too late, we all were. I did not actually get to see the snowy side of the mountain falling, but I could certainly hear it, even feel it on the earth below my feet.

When I looked over there was the unmistakable aftermath of a snow avalanche. The side of the mountain looked like a giant had cut it down. The snow at the bottom rose up hundreds of yards before settling back down to the earth.

"Very common," their guide was telling them. "And very nice that you get to see it."

"Yes, oui!" a woman said in her French accent.

"But maybe it is good that we are not more closer?"

"Oui."

I caught up to Rory, who was resting on a rock.

I sat. He had been there for a moment and already had his breath.

"Well this is a right pain in the bottle, eh?"

I took a few more breaths. "What?"

"Bottle. Bottle and glass?"

"Huh?"

"Bottle and glass. Ass. Cockney rhyming slang mate. You had to have a Tom yet?"

"A Tom?"

"Tom tit. A shit."

"No, I haven't eaten. Who the hell is Tom Tit?"

"Don't know mate, it just means shit."

"You can't just say shit?"

"I mean you could, but that's not how it's done now, is it? Like say you want to call someone an asshole?"

"Ok."

"He's a bit of an elephant, isn't he?"

"An elephant? That doesn't rhyme with asshole." I thought

about it for a minute. "I don't know if elephant rhymes with any-thing."

"No, it's not the first word my son, it's the second. It's the one that we don't say. Like go on up the apples. What we're saying is the old apples and pears, the stairs."

"This is perhaps the worst system of language I have ever heard of."

"It just is what it is mate, isn't it?"

"Wait, so what does elephant remind you of that rhymes with asshole."

"Elephants and castle."

I looked at him. "I need to save my oxygen."

Liam came lumbering up to us. He fell to the ground and rolled around looking for air. After a while he perked up. "I could go for a pig."

I looked at him.

Rory clarified. "Pig's ear. A beer."

I guess when you lose an empire you suddenly have a lot of extra time on your hands.

****

By the time I made it to lunch I had gone through nearly four liters of water. A bit more than a gallon. There was a tarp spread out on the ground. I dropped my pack, took off my shoes, and flopped down for a nap.

"Time for a little Egyptian PT, eh Joel?" Rory called to me as he found his own place on the tarp.

Egyptian? Egyptian what? Camel? Magician? Pyramids?

"I give up." I told him. "What's the second word and what is it supposed to rhyme with?"

"To what mate?"

"Egyptian PT."

"It's not rhyming slang mate, it's just something I picked up in the army, didn't I? Those Egyptians never seen the inside of a weight room in they lives. The closest they ever come to any physical training is taking a good nap."

"Maybe a wank," Liam added.

"Aye, good for the forearms."

The rest of the group had to be fifteen to thirty minutes behind me. I could get in a little rest before lunch.

I again ate my hot bowl of soup. They called it pumpkin soup, but I hadn't seen any pumpkins. I'm pretty sure it was some kind of local squash. At any rate, it was quite good. The soups that these guys made, from scratch and over camp fires, were some of the best I've ever had. My only complaint is I wished there was more soup available. It went down easily, giving me a little bit of food and some more liquid as well. I felt like I could have eaten another bowl, even two, but that option was not on the table. What was on the table was a fantastic lunch spread of chicken, yucca root mixed with a variety of local potatoes, and fried veggies. Normally I'd love this, but my stomach just didn't want it.

I felt hunger and nausea at the same time. I wanted to force a little food into me, I was burning calories at a crazy rate and not eating nearly enough, but I had already vomited twice this morning. I did not need to go for a hat trick. The one bowl of soup would have to do for now.

"You are enjoy you lunch my friends?" Rosel joined us.

We all said that we were.

"How about three cheers for the cooks then lads?" Rory suggested loudly. "Hip hip."

"Hooray!" We all answered.

"Hip hip."

"Hooray!"

"Hip hip."

"Hooray!"

We all clapped and the porters waved. "Thank you boys!" Rory yelled.

"You have in front of you some potatoes," Rosel spoke. "If you will allow for a few minute please I will tell you history of the potatoes. Many peoples when they think of the potatoes they are thinking of what? Of Ireland. But this is not so. The potatoes is of Peru."

I had to admit that I did not know this. I even doubted it at the time. Potatoes are Irish, everyone knows that. But later research showed Rosel to be completely correct.

"All potatoes originate in Peru. It is said by the scientist that the peoples of Peru have the potato as early as five-thousand years before the Christ, and maybe even eight-thousand years before the Christ.

Why? Because the potato is very strong and, how you say..."

"Hardy."

"Yes, I think hardy. So it grow on the side of the hill. But also the potato is growing at very high altitudes without problem.

Now, how many kinds of potatoes there are?

In you country I think maybe there are no so many potato. You go to the store and you see maybe four or five different potato that you can choose from. In Peru we have over four thousand and six hundred different kind of the potato!"

I wondered whose job it was to count potatoes. Some little dude on a llama just spending his entire life traveling out to some guy's remote farm because he claims to have a new potato, then going through his list of four thousand plus other potatoes to see if he remembers trying this one before.

"So how does it come to be that the potato is all over the world and especially in the Ireland? After the Spanish are leaving Peru back for they own country they bring with them the potato. But they bring not so much variety. So you know of in 1845 there is what is known as the potato famine, yes? The potato in Ireland is hit by disease and there is no so much for the peoples to eat. So many peoples die and many other peoples have to move away. I think maybe to you country of United States. Why does this happen? Because the Spanish bring not so many variety of potato home with them. So all potato is the same. If that potato can be affect by disease, then all of the foods for the peoples is gone. But here in Peru if there is a problem with crop then maybe we lose one, two, or even ten variety of potato, but always there is thousands more.

So I think maybe you can see the potato is very important for my peoples the Incan peoples."

"Ok, we go!" The Swedish woman yelled as she and her husband bounced up and down. They had come to America a year ago to compete in some sort of a long-distance trail race in in Colorado. While there, they had become friends with the other couple, the husband and wife from Colorado. I wasn't sure how the younger girl fit in; I think she may have been somebody's niece, but she was faster, younger, and in better shape than any of them. All five had their shoes tied, packs on, and were literally bouncing up and down.

"Just hang on a damned minute," Ed said. "I'm going to the toilet." And off he went. The toilet was actually a small tent, with a portable toilet inside of it. It had some sort of a system where you pump the handle twice, then do your business, then pump it twice more to get a weak flush. Since I had now drank a full gallon of water, yet hardly consumed any real food at all, a tree was all I needed. I understood how that system worked.

"I need a nap." Clint flopped down on the tarp. I felt the same and found my own place on the tarp.

"Little Egyptian PT would do me good. What do you say Liam?"

"Aye, aye."

"We're ready to go!" the man from Colorado told Rosel , a little annoyed.

"I could use a small rest too guys." Abe removed his boots and started massaging his feet.

"Ok, we go, yes!" The Swedish man clapped and tried to get the group to their feet.

I shut my eyes and ignored the arguing and racket around me. As I drifted into a slumber, I faintly heard an old man in a tent yelling. "There's no god damn toilet paper in here!"

****

Rosel was not lying. The climb after lunch was full-on work. Again we leaned into our hiking poles, put one foot in front of the other, and up we went.

We were over fourteen-thousand feet now. The mountain was steep and the oxygen levels were low. I'd move forward twenty steps, then rest. Slowly, without meaning to or trying, I overtook another tour that was trekking up the hill with their guide.

Like us, they had two mules. Both of their mules were being ridden at all times. Someone would get to ride a mule for a while, then they rotated to another person in the group.

Our two mules were well ahead of me now, and both taken, not that I ever would have gotten on one anyhow. Ed rode the first mule. This was fine. He was in his mid-sixties. He served our country honorably for twenty years. If he foolishly thought that he was going to come out here, smoke a pack of cigarettes, then hump a load up a hill like he did in his army days, well, it was laughably ignorant but forgivable.

Abe rode the other mule. The social-justice warrior from Maine didn't have any problem with a me-first attitude when push came to shove. He was thirty-seven years old, thin, and lacking any legit physical problems. This was the issue with our country today, in my opinion. Men like Abe who never got injured on a playground because their parents helicoptered over them. Never drank from a hose. Never rode their bikes without a helmet, built a tree fort, or had their father throw boxing gloves at them and tell them to settle it themselves. Here he was, a perfectly healthy young man, quitting, because the hill was tough. There would not have been a single man in the 1950s who would ever get on that mule. Now America was full of them.

Toxic men saved the world in WW2, landed a man on the moon, and dug the Panama Canal. I might be a toxic male, but I was sick as could be and still walking up a mountain in the Andes.

I looked ahead of me at Rosel. Then I thought about what Celeste had said a couple of days ago. "We're in America! Peru is South America?" Rosel was 5'5" and 130 lbs. He carried a pack that must have weighed double mine. He had two kids, led this hike every week, went to bed an hour after we did and woke up an hour before us. Celeste was right: he was a hell of a lot more American than her unlabeled boyfriend Abe would ever be.

I hiked with one of the three girls from Alabama. She pointed to the peak of Salkantay with her trekking pole.

"It's…" But that was all she could get out.

I agreed; it really was beautiful.

We sat, and gathered our breath. After about a minute she looked at me. "Can I make a confession?"

"Sure."

She looked left and right, as if not wanting anyone else to hear. "I don't really know what Machu Picchu is."

I nodded. There were sixteen people on our trek. To be honest I didn't really get the impression that any of us did. "Well, it's, it's a wonder."

"Yes," she said. "But what is it? I mean, did you read about it at all?"

"A little."

"I didn't. I mean I Googled it the night before our plane left, but I just came because my friends were going. It was just sort of something to do."

"Yeah."

"But I don't think they know what it is either."

I drank some water. "Well, we're in the middle of the Andes. Whatever it is, I think we better hike there."

We leaned into our poles and trekked up some more.

****

"Lovely hikers! Welcome to the top!"

I flopped down. That was it, I had done it. There were still about three more hours to hike today, kilometers to check off, but it would all be downhill, or at least flat, for the rest of the day.

"Maybe you will enjoy here a cup of coca tea while we await for you brothers and sisters to continue their climb to the top of the mountain." I gladly took a cup of liquid cocaine from him. If it will get rid of my headache and give my body energy, I'm all for it. Hell, even if it just warmed me up. It was cold up here!

The weather in the Andes just cannot make up its mind. All day I was constantly shedding and/or adding layers. The sun vs. the shade, the peaks vs the valleys, morning vs afternoon, walking vs resting. We all went from too hot, to too cold, to too hot again. I threw on my outer layer.

I pulled out my cell phone and recorded a babbling selfie video.

"(Gasp for air) Alright kids, here we are (deep breath), six-hundred-and-thirty meters up (totally wrong number), fifteen-thousand feet is what I've heard." Someone in the background references Freddy Mercury and Celeste yells "yeah!" for no reason whatsoever. "We been, ah, hiking up, ah, it took about nine miles of straight-up hiking on jagged rock and, ah, (pause for breath), serious altitude, I'm not going lie to ya, I'm beat."

I wrapped my hands around my tin tea mug and parked myself on a rock.

Looking around, only about half of the group was up here. The five trail runners and the two mule handlers. That was it. I figured I'd have about thirty minutes until Raul, our second guide who always stayed with whoever was in the rear, came up the hill.

Rosel sat next to me. We clicked our tin tea cups together.

"And how are you feeling now my friend?"

"We're at the top of the mountain."

"Yes. But how is you head? And your stomach is still opposite?"

"Told you this morning, I feel good."

"I think maybe this morning you are not telling me that truth. You leave for the bathroom to... How you say? You stomach does not keep the food."

"Vomit."

"Yes. I think you vomit this morning. Then at the lake, I think maybe you are vomit again."

I paused for a moment. "Yeah."

"And your head is miserable the entire way."

"Yeah."

We sipped our coca teas silently for a few minutes. "And at lunch, you do not eat."

"You saw all that, huh?"

"You are no my first hiker to say no to help my friend. On my trail it is my job to see everything, to read all the signs. But, you have made it to the top. I think maybe all the hard parts are done for today and you will not have a problem with another three to four hours of flat walking, yes?"

"No problem at all."

"You will see a really beautiful trail tonight. I think we will walk in the clouds and it will be a new experience for you."

"For sure. How is Ed?"

"Maybe Ed is not so fit for this hike today, but he is no sick. He eats foods and is drinking the water. Now that we are on the top and only maybe eight or so kilometers left, more or minus, I think he will walk."

"Good. And Abe?"

"Abe is no injured, and maybe not so much tired, but he will ride the mule. I think maybe his..." He pointed to his brain.

"His mind?"

"Yes, thank you, his mind. I think maybe his mind is not so strong like you and me."

Like you and me. I liked that.

"Very good my friends!" About thirty minutes later our second guide, Raul, came up the hill with Silent Roberta, the last member of our group. She was from Hungary, or maybe it was Morocco. She didn't speak a word of English, and as far as anyone could tell she also did not understand any Spanish. She certainly never spoke it.

"I think now we have done the hardest part of all of our hikings," Rosel continued. "Not just for today, but also for the rest or our week."

"Yeah, well, we'll bloody see about that."

"Maybe tomorrow is no so bad, then the next day there is some climb…"

"Yep, now we're getting a bit of truth, eh?"

"But not so bad as today. So, we have maybe three or so hours, more or minus, until we get to our campsite. It is what we say Peruvian flat." He made a gradual up and down motion with his hands to indicate gentle rolling hills. That sounded pretty ok with me. "I believe along you way you will see some beautiful thing, Raul and I can tell you all about it and point it out, and you will enjoy very much."

"Sounds good."

"Then, we will be at the campsite. Tonight you will sleep in the tent, very good tent, and two by twos."

"Joel, we doubling up again?" Clint asked me. I gave him a nod.

"The porters have run ahead, both with some mule and also with they own feet, and bring all of you stuff there, you sleeping bags and other things. So the tent will be all put up, the dinner all made. We will remember to say a thank you when we get there, but also of more important in a few days we will remember you porters when it is time to tip. Because here in Peru maybe the salary is no so much and many of these men depend on some small tip in order to have a family."

"No problem there mate. Fair play, isn't that right lads?" We all agreed with Rory.

"Very good. So now I think this is a good spot to have a picture as a family."

Walking again. The soles of my feet hurt, I was hungry, head still hurt, air was still thin, but man it was nice to be on a flat, hard-packed trail!

I fell in with Clint.

"How you feeling?" he asked me.

I shrugged. "Least we're on flat ground now."

"No kidding."

"Could have used more sleep last night."

"That doesn't get to me."

"No?"

"Naw. I'm used to long hours. Now all this walking? Man, my back hurts, hips hurt, knees are starting to hurt…"

"Got any Ibuprofen?"

"No. Do you?"

"Yeah." So we stopped. I gave him two Ibuprofen and we each had some water.

"I'm a union guy," he said as we started back up again. "Steel worker, welder, scrapper, you name it."

"Yeah?"

"Third generation. Grandpa did it, dad did it, now me. It's hard work, but there's money in it if you know what you're doing."

"You know what you're doing?"

"Oh yeah." We walked a bit more. "That's why I was saying I don't mind the hours. I'll go up to Alaska on a contract and work twelves and sevens."

"What's that?"

"Twelve hours a day, seven days a week."

"For how long?"

"Month. Sometimes two."

"Dangerous?"

"It can be. You try to be careful, but yeah."

As we walked the landscape slowly changed. I saw my first small butterfly and it followed along with us for awhile, circling around the colorful hat that Clint had bought in the Cusco markets.

"I took a job once…" Clint went on, "twelves and sevens." But I didn't tell the foreman that I already had another job with my father. So I'd work twelve hours on that job, then drive about an hour and meet my dad for an eight-hour shift, then it would be time to drive back to the first job."

"Hang on here. You're working twelve hours on one job?"

"Yep."

"Eight hours on another job?"

"Yeah."

"And driving two hours every day?"

"It was a bitch."

"That's twenty-two hours a day. When do you sleep?"

"Most sleep you ever get is fifty-five minutes. You get that twice a day. Every time I drive to the next job, I'm an hour early, so I sleep in the car for fifty-five minutes before I go in. With the twelve-hour job I was driving a forklift, I can do that in my sleep, and I basically was. You'd drive a load over to one side of the warehouse, but it might be thirty minutes till the next load is ready, so you sleep a few minutes in the forklift."

"Jesus."

"With my dad's gig, he's a hard ass. But I'd slip off to the bathroom twice a day, put my headphones in, and set my alarm for fifteen minutes. Then I'd sleep on the toilet."

"Aren't you using power tools all the time?"

"Yeah."

"And driving twice a day."

"I'm not saying it's smart, cause it's not, but I could do it."

"Wow."

"So I figured if I could do that sort of thing, or take a contract fracking in North Dakota, or whatever, I'd be able to work maybe four months a year. Rest of the time I could just do stuff like this, sleep, play with my kids, whatever."

"Makes sense."

"I mean, it does on paper. But things never really work out that way, you know?" The butterfly finally left us as we started a steep descent. "I got busted with a hooker. Except she wasn't a hooker of course, she was a cop. Wife didn't like that."

"No, I guess she wouldn't."

"I told her it was the first time. She wanted to believe me, but nobody's that stupid. She knew."

"Yeah."

"Nobody gets busted their first time doing anything."

"Normally not."

"I've probably been with a hundred. It just goes with the job." I didn't say anything. We leaned hard into our trekking poles as we went down the hill. "So now she has a new husband. Got to fight with her all the time just to see the kids."

Going downhill was much easier on the lungs, but it was a different kind of hard for the body. It didn't wear you out like uphill did, but it beat the heck out of you. I'd come thudding down and could just feel the added pressure in my back, ankles, hips, and mostly my knees. The trekking poles helped a lot, but I could tell that a few hours, let alone a few days, of serious downhills was going to take their toll.

Soon we walked into our first look at a cloud forest. The dense fog was everywhere, outlines of trees, mountains behind them, birds flying into and out of the mist, and our trail disappearing before our very eyes.

"So please to welcome my friends to the cloud forest," said Rusel. "What is cloud forest? Cloud forest is actually a tropical forest with a layer of very heavy fogs at the canopy. We find near the mountain ranges, such as here in Peru. The results is a gathering of tree that constantly have a heavy mist around they treetops at all time."

We all snapped some photos.

"Do you know my friends what does the heavy fog? It is working as both a filter of the sunlight and also a constant source of moisture. So it produce an environment that is very unique. Here you will find many mosses and ferns, but also a large number of species that are only live in the cloud forest, both of plant and animal. There is an unknown amount of flower here include many that are yet to be discover. Do you think maybe there are many cures for diseases of the world that may be found here in the cloud forest? I think maybe yes."

"I hate modern medicine," Celeste said.

"It's just a business," Abe agreed. "They don't want to come here to find cures. If they can keep you sick then you stay a customer."

"Ok my friends, we continue our walk. Be on the look for many hummingbird, beautiful frog, and also the seven-foot Peruvian mountain gorilla that eat only gringos." He walked on.

"Wait! What?!" One of the girls from Alabama stopped.

"Haha! Rosel makes joke." We heard his voice ahead in the fog.

We descended through thick brush on both sides. Followed small streams, and heard the birds singing to us as we went.

In time the trail opened up to wide flat fields. Ahead of me I could see Liam walking in and out of the mist.

I heard the horses before I could see them. A few seconds later a pack of twenty to thirty horses emerged from the fog, gently trotting towards me, then passing on either side of me. At the end, their master, an Inca man swinging a rope in a circle, came out of the fog.

"Buenos tardes," he said, and I said it back to him.

****

Around six we staggered into camp. The sun was just starting to set and the entire world had a golden hue to it.

Camp was a beautiful site, nestled in the mountains, flat ground, mules and llamas freely grazing in the distance, and a canopy of fog all around us.

The porters had arrived well before us, our tents were set up, cups of warm coca tea were handed out.

Clint and I stumbled to our tent.

"My friends. We will meet for happy hour in maybe one half hour." We gave Rosel a thumbs up.

It was an amazing setting, yet at the same time my body was shot. My head still ached. The soles of my feet hurt and I was scared I may get blisters. My knees were starting to hurt. After eighteen kilometers, mostly uphill in the sun, I was wobbly on my feet, and now I was starting to get chilly.

"How you feeling?" Clint asked me.

"Same as you I imagine."

"That bad huh?"

I changed my socks, put on my base-layer long johns, put on my llama wool sweater and my REI pull over, and clung to my hot tin mug.

"My legs are sore," Clint said as he made old-man noises every time he moved in the tent.

"Anyone seen Beth?" Rory asked at dinner. I dug into my bowl of soup. It was some sort of quinoa and vegetables.

"These soups are amazing," Abe said. "Have you ever thought about putting out a recipe book for them?"

"You totally could!" one of the girls from Alabama said. "I'd love to be able to make this for my husband."

"You are married?" the trail runner from Sweden asked her.

"No, but one day I hope to be."

Celeste rolled her eyes and said "Oh the great patriarchy strikes again."

"Anyone seen Beth?" Rory asked again.

"You going to eat your soup?" I asked Liam.

"Have at it mate." He pushed his bowl of soup over to me. "I just want some Egyptian PT if I'm honest. Not even hungry."

"Beth's in her tent," one of the trail runners said.

"What, she isn't coming out then?"

"I don't think she feels too good."

"She is a bit opposite tonight?"

"Yeah."

Inside of my tent I quickly drifted off to sleep. The mountains were alive with the sounds of the cloud forest creatures settling in for the night, alpacas and llamas gently grazing, and Rory and Liam, a thin piece of nylon away from me, snoring up a storm.

CHAPTER 5: HIKING, DAY TWO

"Good morning my friends."

Clint and I woke to Rosel's voice outside of our tent.

"I have room service for you. Can I open you tent?"

"Yeah." Clint sat up. "Hang on, I got it." Clint opened the zipper, there was Rosel and Raul with two tin mugs.

"I have coca tea for you."

I sat on top of my sleeping bag, head-to-toe skin-tight, bright white, Under Armour long johns, hair sticking up in every direction, and took my tea. "Thank you."

"So maybe now is a good time to use a toilet, brush you tooth, then I think in fifteen minute, more or minus, you will see a nice sunrise over the mountains, yes?"

"Sounds great, thank you."

"Then we will pack all of our things for the porters, pack separate you day bags, and meet for some breakfast. Ok, I go to the next tent."

These dudes really work hard for their money, and I don't think it is a lot of money.

"Good morning."

One of the three girls from Alabama climbed into our tent and cuddled with Clint.

He looked at me, surprised. I sat in my skin-tight, bright white, long johns, brushing my teeth and spitting into a tin cup.

"Well." I said.

It felt like a complete sentence, so I exited the tent.

With the first glow of light, before the sun had even peeked its tip over the mountains, I was able to see wild horses through the fog. Clear clean land for as long as you can see, a gentle stream, wild horses grazing, and the Andes mountains as the backdrop.

The group was all gathered now.

The sun made its first appearance over the ridge of the mountain and instantly the valley was full of orange light cutting through the fog.

"Wow," somebody whispered.

"It's amazing."

"I'm just happy to be alive," Rory said quietly.

"I know right. Its times like these you can really feel God."

"I'm not talking about that love. Last night I had a tug at fifteen-thousand feet. No oxygen, can't hardly breath, feels like I'm being choked unconscious. I'm worried me mate Liam is going to walk into the tent at any moment so I'm moving me arm as fast as I can, up and down, it's nothing but a wee pecker but it's being stubborn. They say it takes water longer to boil at altitude so I'm thinking maybe this takes longer too? Have to ask Rosel about that. Now me breathing is getting labored, huffing and puffing I is, nearly passed out, saw me dearly departed granddad, he told me what a let down I've always been so I know it's really him now, don't I?"

"Did you really mate?"

"What, see me old granddad?"

"No, have a wank in our tent?"

"Thought I might die mate, you'd come in, find me all stiff! Isn't that right Clint?"

Well, I thought to myself, the sun is up now.

****

I felt good today. Actually good. Not lying good. My headache was gone. My stomach felt fine. Surprisingly every muscle in my body was fresh and ready to go. I felt like me again.

I ate my porridge, and one plate of food. About the same

amount as everyone else. I wanted more, yet I also didn't want to push myself and end up vomiting again.

On the opposite side of the spectrum was Beth.

Beth did not eat. She had not eaten last night either. Her friends, the trail running couple from Colorado, brought her some potage but she waved them off. They tried to give her some coca tea but she would not take that either. Her lips were purple. Not the awful kind of purple that some high-school girls wear when they want you to know that they hate, well, they're not sure what they hate, no, her lips were the awful kind of purple that someone gets when they nearly drown or freeze to death.

Rosel brought out the oxygen tank and she took the mask without complaint.

He next put a pulse oximeter on her finger, a small device that measured both heart rate and the oxygen saturation of her blood. Normal blood oxygen levels, when at sea level, were in the 90s. Anything below 60 is known as hypoxemia, and is considered quite dangerous. Some signs of hypoxemia are shortness of breath along with rapid breathing, rapid heart rate, headache, dizziness, and confusion. Beth checked every box.

I did not hover too closely, so I may be mistaken, but I believe I heard Rosel telling her friends that her oxygen level was somewhere in the 50s.

"You will ride the mule down to our next campsite where the altitude is lower." He was not asking. "Raul will lead the mule and run along you side so all you must do is hold on to the saddle horn. He will also carry the oxygen if you are to need it along the way." She nodded. "Our next campsite is maybe only eight thousand feet so we will test again and maybe you are feeling much better. If not we will radio for the van and Raul will go with you to the hospital."

He then yelled something to Raul in Quechua and they were off.

Our campsite may have just been tents, but it did have one permanent structure. A concrete block building with two flush toilets. I would be sure to use this prior to leaving.

I opened the door to the first stall. It was not terribly clean, but it did have a first-world style toilet. It did not have a seat or any toilet paper. I was holding two napkins that I snagged at breakfast, but more paper would always be welcome. I decided to check out stall number two.

Stall two was more or less the exact same, so I stayed. I pulled my pants all the way down by my ankles, squatted about a foot above the toilet, and, without any warning, exploded.

I missed. I mean I really missed. It wasn't full-on diarrhea but it certainly wasn't solid, and it wasn't in the bowl. Like a blind man at a shooting range, I was all over the place. I killed the back of the toilet, the wall, and the floor on both sides. There was no running water in here, and I had only two small napkins. I needed both of them to clean myself, nothing to spare for the floor.

I used the napkins, pulled up my pants, and glanced out the tiny front window. There was a porter heading my way with some meager cleaning supplies! Quickly I ducked into the first stall, the semi-clean one, the one I had not used. I locked the door.

He opened the door to the main building. He tried to open the door to my stall, where I hid. I said something quickly and he apologized in Spanish then opened the door to the second stall. I don't know what he said in Quechua, but one does not need to understand a language to know swear words when you hear them.

I took a piss in my stall and flushed the toilet. I stepped out. He was there, still staring at the mess in the other stall. I looked over his shoulder.

"Uh!" I said, sounding surprised and disgusted. I then made a gesture to show what he already knew, I just came out of the other stall, the clean one, this mess couldn't be from me.

I felt terrible.

****

"Ready!" the Swedish man said. Then he and his wife jogged

off down the trail. The couple from Colorado quickly followed them.

"I've just about had it with that lot," Rory said to me. "It's not a bloody race now, is it?" I couldn't have agreed more.

We set off at a walk. We had twenty-four kilometers to cover today, or in American, roughly fifteen miles. Rosel told us that it was "Peruvian flat" meaning a little up, then a little down. But overall it would be mostly down. Tonight we would camp at about eight-thousand feet, so we should go mostly down, which was obviously less work than up. Also the air would have a little more oxygen in it every kilometer that we clicked off.

Rosel promised us a nice hike. I looked forward to it and I got to walking. Abe rode the mule.

In the morning we went roughly seven or eight miles downhill. As we hiked lower and lower the climate and environment changed quickly. When we woke in the morning it was quite chilly, but now we were hiking into the tropical rain forest. We all stripped off as many layers as we could. The air was hot and humid, but the canopy of trees was lovely. The streams bubbled by us, and the birds all sang their good-morning songs. So did the lads from the UK:

"Do, do, come have a drink or two, down at the old Bull and Bush! Bush! Bush!

Come, come, come and make eyes at me, down at the old Bull and Bush.

Come, come, drink some port wine with me, down at the old Bull and Bush!

Da, da, da, da, da..."

"Fancy a drink or ten tonight Joel?"
"A drink, sure. One. Maybe two."
"Ah, you lot can't hold your liquor, can you?"
"Don't know, not going to try."
"Lightweights, our colonial cousins, eh Liam?"
"Aye, aye."

"You may have invented it, but we perfected it," Ed said from about ten feet behind us.

"How about you then, have a beer with the lads sir?"

"I'll have a beer with you, but don't you call me sir, I worked for a living."

"A sergeant then was it?"

"That's right. Twenty years, honorable discharge in 1995."

"Good man."

"So it's a restaurant staffed entirely by returning citizens."

"Returning from where?" I asked Abe. A porter with a heavy pack on his back lead Abe, who sat on a mule, as I walked besides them.

"So the States has the highest incarceration level of any nation, right? And we know that law enforcement disproportionately and unfairly targets people of color."

"So the entire restaurant is run by ex-cons?"

"Returning citizens."

"And you own it?"

"No, it wouldn't be right for me to own it."

"Why not?"

"Well as a white male…" He trailed off as if the rest were obvious.

"I don't follow."

"It wouldn't be right for me to hold a position of authority over people of color, especially after they have been victims of an oppressive system."

"Sure. Or you could view them as people who rightfully did time for committing a crime."

"So Celeste is the owner. I bus tables. Celeste has actually promoted quite a few of the returning citizens to positions of authority above me," he said proudly.

"And it's successful?"

"What's that?"

"The restaurant."

"Define successful."

"The restaurant is making money."

"Money, no. And we did have a set back when one of our returning partners borrowed a large sum without Celeste's consent."

"Shocking."

We walked across a group of logs that were laid out to make a bridge over a smaller river. Abe gripped the saddle horn with both hands as a small person of color continued to carry his things and lead his mule.

"So..." I went on. "If you don't mind the question, if you're not making money, how do you stay in business? Or afford a trip to Peru?"

"We define success in other ways."

"Yes, ok, but the landlord still wants the rent I imagine."

"Celeste and I run a nonprofit. We're both lucky enough to come from privilege so our network keeps the nonprofit afloat."

"So your parents paid for your trip to Peru?"

"Um, no. Family donated to our nonprofit?"

"Which you then used to vacation in Peru."

"We believe that travel broadens the mind. The States could be much more accepting of other cultures."

"So your parents paid for the trip, and they got a tax write off for it."

****

"Left or right?"

"I have absolutely no idea."

A group of five of us stood at a fork in the trail. Left went down the mountain. Right was fairly flat. Left seemed to go towards the stream, and we remembered that we're supposed be camping near a stream tonight, but what stream? And it was way too early for camping. Right seemed to go into a series of small buildings, maybe somebody's home or a few homes. That didn't seem correct either.

"Has anyone seen Rosel?"

"I haven't seen him in hours."

"Well we can't just wait for Raul, he took Beth ahead on the mule. There's nobody bringing up the rear today."

"Ed and Alice are back there."

"I'm Alice," said one of the girls from Alabama.

"Sorry. Ed and the other one. What's your friend's name?"

"Kathy."

"Ed and Kathy are still back there."

"And silent Roberta."

"Oh yeah, I forgot all about her."

"We're going to have to wait for them before we go."

"Sure, but go where."

We all just stood there. Two perfectly good trails. No signs. No guides. So, we all just stood there.

"Who speaks the best Spanish here?" I asked.

"Abe."

"Abe rode ahead on the mule. Here, in this group, who speaks the best Spanish here?"

"You."

I looked around. Nobody else spoke a word. To say I spoke *the best* Spanish is not correct in any circumstance. I spoke the worst Spanish, but the others spoke none.

"Well that's not good news for us. Ok, I'm going to walk over to those buildings, can't be more than a quarter mile. I'll try to talk to someone there and see if our group came through this way."

So off I went. I just hoped whoever I found actually spoke Spanish, because I sure as heck didn't speak Quechua.

I came to a small building, a shack, full of goods that campers and hikers would want. A trailside mini mart.

"Pringles?" The old Inca lady waived a can of pringles at me.

"No I don't want to buy any Pring…" But I did. I did want Pringles. "What else you got?" She didn't understand a word I was saying, but I stuck my head into the small window. "Snickers, dos, y Pringles, si, y tambien Gatorade."

She reached for the red Gatorade.

"No, green, verde. That one. Si."

She handed me the can of Pringles, two Snickers bars, and a green Gatorade.

"Cuantos?"

It came out to just over ten bucks in American money, a steep price, but I didn't care. This was hardly a spot where the Walmart truck made regular deliveries. Some poor schmuck had to walk two days into town, load up his mule, and hike all the way back here just to fill the store. If they had a little markup, they earned it.

I hiked back to the group.

"Is that the right way?"

"Don't know."

"What do you mean you don't know?"

"Didn't ask."

"Why didn't you ask?"

"Forgot."

"Huh?"

"They have Pringles."

"Pringles?"

I showed the group my can of Pringles. "Pringles, snickers, twix, soda, Gatorade, fresh water, jerky, peanuts..."

"Ok, I'm sold."

The group picked up their packs and hiked to the store.

This time I asked the lady, in very bad Spanish, if our group had come through here earlier. She said, without a doubt, that they had. Of course, it occurred to me that a number of groups come through there every day, and we all look the exact same. How in the hell would she know if it was *our* group? Still, it stood to reason that the store would be set up on the trail, and thus I assumed that we must still be going the correct way. We waited for Ed, one girl from Alabama, and silent Roberta, then we continued down the trail.

****

Only about a kilometer later we walked up to our porters, all set up for lunch.

"Ok, we eat?" The Swedish man jumped to his feet.

"Now just hang on a minute Ludwig," Ed dismissed him.

"I am not Ludwig. Who is Ludwig?"

"I'm going to sit down, rub my feet, use the toilet. It's going to be a few minutes. Just keep your knickers on."

"I do not wear knickers. This is German."

As we rested, Rosel and the porters played soccer. I found it every bit as obnoxious as Rosel playing the flute while hiking uphill. I am in shape man. I felt strong today, no excuses, yet after a six-hour morning hike I had zero energy or desire to play soccer.

At lunch I ate. I mean I really ate. It was the first time I was able to get more calories into my body than I was burning.

Lunch started with some kind of crackers and guacamole. I inhaled my portion. Next came the hot bowl of soup. Locro de papas, potato soup. Finished that.

The porters then cleared the plates and brought out chicken, rice, yucca, and veggies. I ate three heaping plates.

"This afternoons we will be join with section of the very original Inca Trail. This parts that we walk will be built by Incan peoples over six-hundred years ago. So we must work hard to both enjoy the trail and yet at the same time the Peru government has responsibility no to allow too many peoples on the trail every day so they do not get ruin. So now it is limit to only five hundred peoples per day, include the guide like me and the porter. Also there is no more allowed the mule. So Mr. Abe I think that you will be strong enough to walk."

Abe exhaled a little bit. I shut my eyes and shook my head in disgust, not caring if he saw or not.

"Also what this means is three of our porter who is working with the mule, they are no more for this trip. So now, after lunch, we are saying goodbye to them and also maybe to give a tip. What you think is good tip is up to you each, but I am suggest that it is twenty each."

"Twenty dollars? That's it?" Ed asked.

"You are in Peru now Mr. Ed. Twenty sols, everything money is in sols." Rosel then excused himself.

"Twenty sols? That's like…" He paused, tried to calculate it in his head, then pulled out his phone. "Where's the calculator on this damned thing?"

"It's a bit more than six bucks," I told him.

"Six bucks? Six bucks! Well I'm not in for six bucks, these guys are working their asses off."

"What do you suggest?" Abe asked him.

"Hell, I don't know. But how am I going to look these men in the eye and give them six bucks?"

"So…"

"Russel said what?"

"His name is Rosel?" Celeste corrected him.

"That we should pitch in twenty sols each. Well here's forty." Ed put forty sols on the table. "And even that feels really cheap. Really cheap."

"You can't just do that." Celeste looked at him and shook her head. "You'll ruin their local economy."

"What are you talking about?"

"They'll become dependent on Western money?"

"Sweetheart, they're already dependent on American money. Look around you!"

"You are such an imperialist!"

"You do what you want with your money, I'll do what I want with mine."

"With no care for the common good."

"That's it, I'm done. Forty sols."

"Then I'm done too. I'm not tipping. That way it will average out to twenty each."

"Oh yeah?" Ed opened his wallet back up. "Here's forty more!" He put forty more on the table for a total of eighty. "Who's in?"

"I'll go forty." Clint told him.

I did too and the others all followed.

Abe started to get out his wallet.

"What are you doing?" Celeste glared at him.

"Well I…"

"Oh no you're not!"

Abe put away his wallet. Celeste got up and stormed out. Abe meekly followed. At the last moment, after she had turned the corner, he darted back and put twenty sols on the table, motioning for all of us to stay quiet. He turned to rush after her, then spun around again and placed down another twenty, making his total forty just like the rest of us. Like an insane mime he frantically waved at all of us to swear to absolute silence, then he spun and rushed after Celeste.

****

By mid-afternoon we found ourselves insanely spread out. The trail runners, who now only numbered four, must have been a solid mile in front of me. Ed and a few others may have been a mile behind me.

When the day had started I actually jogged a little. The trail runners were jogging, a few of the Alabama girls tried to stay with them, so when I came to the gradual downhills I jogged. Then I stopped. I said to myself "What the hell am I doing?" I'm on a trek. I'm here to see things. They were seeing absolutely nothing.

So that was it. They ran around the corner and I let them.

The landscape today was more of a cliff walk. I don't want to make it out to be scarier than it was, but there was for sure an element of danger. It was mostly a downhill walk, or Peruvian flat, along the edge of a cliff. Many spots were nice thick paths that you could drive an ATV down, but there were some spots that were as narrow as two or three feet. It was enough room to walk, but not a whole lot to spare.

If you were to fall... well it wasn't a death drop, but it was a steep hill that you would slide, or worse bounce, down. Eventually you would get tangled up on some thick bushes and stop. You may end up twenty or fifty yards down, and you'd almost for sure have broken something. I decided it would be best not to slip and fall off the edge.

One of the girls from Alabama decided the same thing, but she was much more adamant about it than I was.

"Best way to tackle it is to just turn your mind off and walk," I told her. But this was not going to happen. Her mind was on, and her legs were not interested in walking. She pressed her body against the side of the cliff and whimpered as she shuffled slowly, almost in tears.

"Ok." It had been nearly a full kilometer since our last cliff, but now we were facing our narrowest trail yet, two feet in some spots, only eighteen inches in others. "Give me your bag. I'm going to carry both bags across, then I'll come back for you. You can hang on to my shoulders and we'll walk across it together." With no other real choice, she nodded.

We kept this system up all afternoon.

At some point she and I sat to have some water and snacks. There we waited for the rest of the group.

There was now a pack of seven of us walking at a moderate pace, chatting and stopping whenever we wanted to photograph something. This was trekking. My only complaint was there was no guide. I had many questions, all of which would remain unanswered.

A few more kilometers and we came upon a small rest area with benches in the shade and a toilet. The front pack of our group was waiting for us there, had likely been waiting a long time, as soon as we showed up they jumped to their feet and pulled on their packs.

"Ok! We go?" Ludwig (as Ed called him) said excitedly the second we walked into the rest area.

"What took you so long?" The women from Colorado

asked cheerfully. "Ludwig was first."

"Well…" He looked bashful as he accepted his imaginary first-place ribbon. "But we were right on his heels. Clint you were right behind us for a while. What happened?"

"I like to take pictures," Clint said dryly, annoyed.

"Ok, we go?" Ludwig said again and jogged off with the others behind them. Rosel picked up his pack and ran too; he had to show them which way to go.

"I'm getting bloody tired of that lot," Rory said for the second time today.

We had no choice but to keep walking. No water break, no toilet, no snacks, no pulling our boots off for ten minutes, no questions answered or explanations of what we were seeing today.

A group from France came into the rest area, all together as a group, and sat down. Their guide pointed out some wild growing fruits and spoke about them in Quechua while another man translated to French.

I was pissed off.

****

Clint and I walked, a decent gap between us and the others.

"So what was that this morning? With that girl from Alabama, April?"

"Dude, I don't know! She just came in the tent, and…"

"Yeah!"

"Yeah!"

"Anything interesting after I left?"

"Not really. We kind of cuddled for a few minutes then it was time for the sunrise so…"

"Well listen, you have to figure out how to throw me out tonight."

"Yeah."

We walked silently for a bit. The walk was easy now, flat, with the last of the cliffs safely behind us.

"You have any condoms?"

"Yeah, I got some in my pack, give you one tonight. We have to figure out how to get me out of your room."

"Wait…" Clint said. "Is she April or Alice?"

"Um. We'll she's not Mary."

"No, Mary has the dark hair. But the one that came into our tent this morning, is her name April? Or Alice?"

"Ah… huh?"

A few hours later we came to our camping place for the evening, Hobbit Huts!

Two rows of huts were built into the side of the hill, with little round doors, just like the hobbit huts in the movie *Lord of the Rings*. The roofs had layers of real grass growing on top of them. The interiors had two beds, a bathroom, and a little back door. Clint opened it.

"Joel! Check this out!"

I stepped out onto a small back porch with him. We were overlooking the Urubamba river. Between us and the river was a swimming pool and two hot tubs! This was nothing like what the original Incas lived in, and I couldn't care less, it was awesome!

"I'm going for a beer in the lodge with the guys." Clint told me. "Coming?"

"I'm going to hit the shower."

And I did. The shower was perfect. Maybe not the best shower I'd ever been in, but one of the more welcome ones for sure. And it was hot, not luke warm, or hot for just a minute or two, but actually hot. Hot to the point where you had to mix in cold water or you'll burn yourself, hot that didn't quit. I stood there. After I had stood there for a long time, I then stood there some more.

"You have good hiking today?" Rosel asked me as we ran into each other outside of my hobbit hut.

"To be honest, no, I did not."

"Oh."

"And I don't want you to take this wrong, because I like you, I really do. I think you're a good guy."

"Ok."

"But the problem was you."

"Oh."

"I didn't sign up for some kind of mountain race. I'm sick of this 'Let's go! Let's go!' bullshit."

"Yes."

"And this isn't just me saying this, believe me, I had seven people today tell me the same thing."

"I understand. But they move very fast and..."

"They move at the speed you allow them to move. You're leading this trek."

"Yes, but they want to go, go, go."

"Who is in charge? You are in charge or they are in charge?"

"I am in charge."

"Then you need to be in charge. They want to run, it's your job to say no."

"Yes."

"Or let them run! I don't give a damn. Let them run ahead, and maybe they find the lodge and maybe they don't, that's not my problem. But we hired you to take us on a trek."

"Yes."

"And that's the speed we're moving at. And I know that we're not moving too slowly because we passed another group on the way here."

"Yes."

"They're not seeing a damned thing. They're not seeing any of the birds, flora... I mean they're just learning nothing. And I don't care, if they want to run through the entire experience that's fine, but I don't. I didn't sign up for a race, I signed up for a trek."

"I understand."

"What's the motto of your company? 'It's not about the destination, it's the journey'."

"Yes, the journey."

"If all they wanted to do was get to Machu Picchu fast they could have taken the train. That's fast!"

"You are right my friend, I'm sorry."

"You're a good guy man..."

"Thank you."

"I mean it. But there's more to this than just not having a real tour today. Where are you with the oxygen if someone else needed it?"

"You are right."

"Where are you with the first-aid kit?"

"Yes."

"What if someone slipped over the side today? That has to happen. That's a two-man job to go get someone, but where are you? If you're around you can radio one of the porters, but without you that means that I'm going down that hill to rescue someone with Clint, or Liam, or Rory. And we'll do it man, but we're not cut out for it. You grew up in these mountains, I can't move here like you can. I'd do it, I'd go down that hill after someone, but it's a serious safety risk having our group all spread out like we were today."

"Yes. Tomorrow I will promise you it will not be so. Thank you my friend for this. I am always learning."

"Ok. I'm sorry. Lo siento. I like you Rosel ..."

"Thank you."

"It's just today..."

"Yes."

"Ok."

We shook hands. He took it so well. I believed in what I had said, but I replayed the conversation many times in my mind in the hope that I was being firm without yelling, cursing, or otherwise being an asshole. He was such a good guy.

****

"Hey Supergirl." Beth sat at dinner. Raul had brought her here, to the lower altitude, on the mule, given her oxygen, and monitored her all day. She didn't look great, but she certainly looked better. "How are you?"

"Ah, I just can't... I can't believe this is happening to me. This sort of thing doesn't happen to me."

"I understand completely."

"I'm just so used to my body working. Doing exactly what it's supposed to do."

"Me too." She picked at her food. "They checked all your oxygen levels and all that?"

"Yeah. I'm doing better. Not where a healthy person should be, but better." She paused. "Oxygen's in the low 80s. Where's yours?"

I paused. I actually thought about lying and lowering my scores a little. Rosel had come around and checked all of us. My oxygen was 93 and my pulse was down in the low 70s, both numbers were on par with the porters. Instead of lying, I just skipped the question. "Can you eat?"

"Maybe a little."

"When I was sick I could still eat soup. Eat yours. When you're done tell me if you want mine too. I can double up on the solid foods now."

In the evening we all sat in the hot tub, listened to the Urabamba river, and looked at the stars. Rory bought a pitcher of some sort of tropical drinks for all of us.

A few moments later Rosel joined us. "It is ok my friends?"

"Yes!"

He climbed into the hot tub. "Very nice." Somebody handed him a drink. "Oh, thank you, super hikers! Cheers!"

"So..." Rosel went on, "I think maybe tonight we are a little more awake than last night. You are in hot bath, you have some drink, and now maybe it is good time to learn something about Inca constellations, yes?"

"Absolutely."

"So to start you will notice what is much bright down here compare to you home, the Milky Way. You will see here the large glowing band that drifts all across the middle of the sky."

Ed poured another round of cocktails and passed them out.

"Rosel?" He held one for our guide. "Ah, si, gracies my friend." He took a sip, approved, and nodded at Ed. "Next, we will see here, the Southern Cross. When you are navigate in the North the men of the sea use what? The North Star. But here, in the South of the Earth, men uses the Southern Cross. It is what is seen on the flag of Brazil, New Zeeland, and Australia even today."

I sunk further down into the warm water, letting it run over my shoulders, and leaned my head back to look at the stars.

"So now, what about the constellation of the Inca? In the sky the Mayu, the Milky Way, stretch across the sky. The Inca Empire stretch from Ecuador to Chile. The Mayu is the life-giving river of the sky just like the Urubamba River here in the Sacred Valley is its counterpart here on the Earth."

I took a drink.

"Inside of the Mayu is dark spaces. The Inca sees not only in the sky the stars to make up constellations, but also the dark spaces. In the dark spaces you can see many animal that come to drink from the Mayu. If you look here..." we followed his finger up "you will see the most important of the dark constellations, Yacana, the two llamas."

He pointed out the shape of a mother llama with a baby llama suckling at her breast. He then also showed us other dark spaces in the Milky Way that made the shapes of a fox, a snake, and a toad.

Ed passed around more drinks. He was on a mission to show the two guys from the UK that they were amateurs.

"Even though we worship the dark constellations still we are always the children of what? The sun. So every year we have the festival of Inti Edmi celebrate on the winter solstice, the shortest day of the year. This year it will be very soon I think, on June 22. It is both celebration of the Sun God, and also of the New Year."

"Shooting star!" Abe called out and we all had a chance to see it.

"Yes, very nice. So how is the Inti Edmi celebrate? It last

for nine days with many colorful dances and processions, the sacrifice of llama, and yes my friends, even the sacrifice of some childrens."

"Jesus Christ," Ed said.

Celeste shot him a look to let him know that he was being very disrespectful.

"Well it's god damn barbaric."

"It is a long time ago Mr. Ed. So after the Spanish comes they ban the ceremony."

"Thank god."

"You are such a toxic male," Celeste mumbled with utter disgust.

"It's toxic males, sweetheart, that keep you safe in the good old United States of America so you can prance around your high-priced universities and tell each other how virtuous you are."

"Alright guys…" Abe tried to cut them off. "We're just looking at the stars."

"No I don't like that either," one of the girls from Alabama said. "It's not good to kill children."

"Including the unborn," a second girl from Alabama added.

"Amen," said the third.

"My body, my choi…"

"Oh your body my ass!" Ed yelled. "It's not just your…"

"Please, everyone!" Abe said again.

"You probably voted for Trump." Celeste glared at him.

"You're god damn right I did!"

"Guys!" Abe shouted. "We're in the middle of the Andes. Sitting in a hot tub. We just had an amazing hike, and Rosel is trying to tell us about the Incan stars. Can he do that please?"

"Yes."

"By all means."

"So I think maybe Mr. Abe is right. There is much debate and anger everywhere and it is best for all of us to leave it someplace else. This is once in a lifetime journey for you and it is best to enjoy with friend. So even though maybe we are not all friend elsewhere, here we must be as brother and sister. Yes?"

There was silence for a moment. Then Ed spoke. "Celeste, you're empty, let me get you a refill."

She glared at him for a moment, then softened a bit and passed him her cup. He poured her another drink.

"Thank you."

"You're welcome."

It wasn't really an apology from either of them, but it was good enough.

CHAPTER 6:
DAY THREE

"I think I can make it if we put my bag on one of the mules."

"Unfortunate the mule is finish now. They are no allowed on this part of the trails."

Beth was silent for a few minutes. "I really don't want to drop out."

"You health is more or minus right now. I will not say no, but maybe it is best if you ride the van to Machu Picchu."

She looked devastated. I could tell that the next words to come out of her mouth were very hard for her. "Maybe one of the porters could carry my bag?" She looked up hopefully. "I'm sorry. I'll even tip more. I think I could make it if I didn't have to carry my bag."

"I would do this thing for you. But my bag is fifty-five pound. All the porter bag is fifty-five pound. It is the most that is allow by Peru law. You bag is maybe only twenty-five more pound, more or minus, and I would do this for you but I cannot. If the marshal, you know the marshal he come around the tours on the trail often, and if he see me or one of my porter with more than fifty five pound than I lose my license to tour."

Beth nodded.

"I'll do it," I said. "I'll carry your pack."

"You are no more opposite?" Rosel asked me.

"I'm perfect."

"Yes, but maybe it is difficult for you?"

"It won't be difficult. Her pack and mine together will still only be fifty-five pounds, probably even less."

"Yes, but maybe we have been in this mountain all of our life."

"I'll be fine."

When I stood up from breakfast, I was stiff as a board. Back was frozen in place, knees were shot, ankles refused to rotate. I Frankensteined my way back to our hobbit hut.

"You got any Ibuprofen?" I asked Clint. I couldn't find mine.

"Yeah, I borrowed a bunch from Ed. That guy has a whole pharmacy with him."

He fished two out and I chugged them down with a liter of water. I was trying to get a full liter into me every morning before we started hiking, just to start off with a good level of hydration. Normally it meant just sitting there and chugging a full bottle whether I wanted it or not.

We picked up our packs and headed out to the main lawn near the start of the trail.

"Ok!" Ludwig jumped up. "We go?"

"No so yet. First we will stay here ten minute, more or minus, so entire group has time to use toilet, stretch, and fill all water bottles." Good start Rosel, I thought to myself. "Today Raul will go in the lead. He will walk and nobody is to pass him. I will stay in the rear, with the entire group always within a close site of each other. I think this is how it is going to be, and no arguments." That a boy.

****

With my pack on my back, and Beth's on my front, I was still surprisingly comfortable. The weight didn't bother me at all. Only minor complaint is they really insulated me, front and back, so I was sweating like a high-pressure shower head. I made sure to drink even more, which in turn of course made me sweat more.

I had stretched out prior to the hike, and the Ibuprofen was kicking in. I felt really good, really strong. My headaches and altitude sickness were well behind me. Today would be an easy and beautiful walk of only twelve kilometers, just seven to eight miles.

Beth lagged a bit behind the rest of the group, but Rosel and I stayed with her the whole way. Raul did a good job of walking, then finding places to pause until we caught up.

To Beth's amazing credit, she kept walking. She was obviously only at fifty percent, but she possessed a strong mind. Willpower is what it takes to get up a hill. At some point everyone gets tired. Some people just keep taking steps. Others ride a mule.

"Please have a try my friends." Rosel handed us each a fruit which looked like a type of orange with a handle. "This is the Granadilla of Peru. First, is very easy to peel and not stick to you hands." He peeled the orange part of his fruit back, revealing a weird white soft second layer. We did the same. "Now to make a small hole at the top." He peeled a bit of the white layer away from the top. "And squeeze the fruit into you mouth."

The insides looked like something out of an alien movie. Translucent jelly fruit full of seeds.

"The seeds?" Beth asked.

"Yes, you chew and eat."

"Can you eat?" I asked her.

"I think I can have some fruit."

"Good."

We squeezed out the weird jelly full of seeds and chomped them up. It didn't look like anything I was used to, but it tasted just fine.

We continued our walk, through a tropical forest, on nice hard packed trails.

"So you know how is freeze dried, yes? This was invented by the Inca."

Rosel had shown Beth and me how to spot natural-growing strawberries by finding first their little white leaves on the side of the hills, then moving the leaves aside to find the berries. We both now had a handful of small strawberries as we walked and talked.

"The three staple crops of the Inca were the corn, potato, and quinoa. I think maybe now you have also the quinoa in America, no?"

"Yeah. Health food."

"Yes, is very good and is main food of the Inca. The quinoa seeds was used to make cereal, flour, and soups."

"Take some more water," I told Beth.

"I'm ok."

"The more you drink the more hydrated you are and the less I weigh. Take some water." She did.

"The Inca peoples grow more foods than they needed. Stored food was dried and keep in special buildings. Because they lived high in the Andes, where it is often much cold, it was easy to dry food. First, they stamped on it until all of the water was out. Then, they left it out to freeze. Finally, they left it out in the sun to finish drying. So you see, Inca is the first to invent the freeze drying and preserving of foods so we can eat also in the winter."

****

"Doing the gentlemanly thing and carrying Beth's bag for her then, are you Joel?" Rory asked me when we caught up with the group. They were resting at a minor ruin along the trail.

"I am."

"Good man. Let me know if you want to switch off."

I pulled Beth's pack off and walked it over to her. She sat about ten feet away from the guys.

"How are you feeling?"

She just nodded.

"Have some more water."

She nodded again. I walked back to the guys, took my own pack off, and sat.

"Two packs up the hill." Rory whistled. "He's doing some work, isn't he Liam?"

"He is mate."

"Looking for a reward then, are you Joel?"

"Alright." I held up my hand in a stop gesture.

"What, you don't fancy girls mate?"

"I fancy girls just fine."

"Nothing wrong with being a poof, is there Liam?"

"Wouldn't know."

"Aye, aye, me neither that's a fact."

"Hysterical. You two should tour the middle-school circuit, you'd be a big hit."

"You don't fancy her then?"

"She's a nice girl."

"Not a looker?"

"She's perfectly good looking."

"So what's the problem my son?"

"There's no problem. She's sick, I'm not, I'm just being a decent guy."

"Oh bullocks. Ask her for a reach around."

"I'm not asking anybody for...!" I lowered my voice. "I'm not asking anybody for a reach around. Look, just keep your voice down ok. I don't mind you busting my balls but keep your voice down. She would feel really awkward and embarrassed if she heard this."

"Alright, steady on."

"I'd carry your bag if you were sick."

"Nobody carries me kit." He lay back on his pack and shut his eyes. "But if you did, I'd have the common courtesy to give you a reach around."

"So my friends, we are here at the Llactapata ruins. It is a spot where we stop and have a rest on our journey to Machu Picchu. And why? Not only is it because we are tired and desire some water. No. Because Llactapata, which in Quichua mean High City, is build as a place for the Inca peoples to stop and have a rest on they way to Machu Picchu. So you see, I think it is good that we stay here for a few moments and rebuild our strength."

We all sat. In front of us were a series of stone walls that made up the foundations for a cluster of homes hundreds of years ago.

"Here we can see that the Incas had a urban center, homes, places for the growings of foods, and a cemetery.

So how much do we really know about Llactapata? I think maybe there is much still to be discover. The Inca made hundreds of roads and this Inca Trail that we travel now was only restore by the Peruvian government in 2003. So now more scientist will come, and much more will be discover about Llactapata in the future."

****

"Look here my friends!"

We were back on the trail. The main group walked ahead. Beth walked slowly, but she was still walking. Very tough girl.

I followed Rosel 's finger through the leaves and saw a very small bright blue frog!

"It is the poison dart frog. Most frog is what? Green and maybe brown. Why? To hide. If can blend into brush then it is no easy for other animals to see and ultimate to eat. But this frog is in many bright color. Blue, yellow, orange, and red. How come this is? Because the frog wants to be see. He is saying, I am poison, you do not want to eat me, you do not want to touch me. Look how small the frog is. But in this one little frog we have enough poison to kill as many as ten fully grown men."

"Wow." I handed Beth her pack so she could get her phone and take a picture.

We walked on. "So in addition to poison the Inca fights much with the club. This lead to many injury of the skull. Even six-hundred years ago the Inca have doctor who are very advance at skull surgery. We have now found hundreds of skull where a doctor has drill a hole into the man's head."

"Oh my god."

"Don't worry Miss Beth, you headache is no so opposite

that I will need to operate."

"No, it is not."

"But if it was, what is the successful rate of this surgery? Scientist tell us that over eighty percent of the patients live. Now to compare this to the doctors in your United States? Over hundreds of year later, during you civil war, the American doctors do the same surgery but only fifty percent of the patient live. So you see the Inca doctor is very advance."

We came out of the forest and met up with the rest of the group in a small village. It was a good spot to rest, have some water, and use a tree.

Ludwig, I never did learn his real name, Ed just named him Ludwig one day and that's what the rest of us called him, seemed to have resolved himself to the fact that we were not in a race. I even saw him bring out a camera.

The village was full of loose dogs, loose turkeys, and loose children.

"That's terrible," one of the girls from Alabama said.

"What?"

She pointed to one of the dogs. It was missing an ear. All the dogs had an injury or two. We saw a dog with a limp, a dog with open wounds, a lot of dogs with minor cuts. They lived, slept, and obviously fought, on their own out here.

"It's a tradeoff, isn't it?" Abe said to her.

"What is?"

"Well, in some ways the dogs here have a much rougher life. They have to fend for themselves. Catch their own food, or rummage through the garbage."

"Why can't the people be nicer to them?"

"But on the flip side, they get to run and be free all day. None of these dogs are chained in a backyard or locked in a tiny apartment."

"I guess. I don't know."

Rory stood next to a small wood box, the lady inside was selling the typical trail foods.

"Oy, Joel! How do you say apple?"

"Manzana. But my pronunciation is probably terrible. Just point."

"Man-lasagna" Rory said to her. She just stared at him. "Apple." This time he pointed. "Oy, who else wants an apple then? Or a soda, I'm buying."

Rory bought about ten apples and passed them out to the group.

"These guys don't have the slightest idea what they're doing." Clint said to me. I followed his eyes to a group of three men that were erecting some sort of two story building out of concrete blocks. Even to my completely untrained eye, they looked like they didn't have the slightest idea what they were doing. They were just laying down a block, slapping on some mortar, then laying the next one down. I'm not saying I could do any better, but there's a reason why nobody would ever give me a builder's license in America.

"You know concrete?"

"I'm not a master with it, I'm an iron worker by trade, but I certainly know more than they do. That building's coming down, it's just a question of when."

It was crazy when I thought about it. The ancient Inca put up stone buildings, without any mortar, that were built to withstand earthquakes. And they lasted, still standing today. The modern Inca was shown how to build "correctly" per Western standards, and now he was a third-rate builder at best. I hated to sound too much like Abe, but just like a broken clock, he was right twice a day.

As we continued to walk through the village we came to a small circular pit with a three foot wall around it. Bleachers surrounded the pit.

"So here we have the area for fighting the cock."

"Nope." One of the Alabama girls walked away.

"In Peru the cock fighting is very popular and it is totally legal. So maybe in other countries you see many crime or bad peoples at the cock fight and it is much danger, but here it is just like to watch football. Everybody come, even the childrens."

"You can see here is the champion of this town."

A large black cock with a read head strutted around. He was long and lean, fast looking, aggressive.

"He looks like Deontay Wilder," I said.

"That is so racist." Celeste shook her head.

"How is it racist?"

"It just…" she paused, "is."

"Ed, tell me that cock doesn't look like Deontay Wilder!"

"It does."

"Well of course you would think so."

"He does look a bit like him actually," Clint chimed in.

"Do you even know who Deontay Wilder is?" I asked Celeste.

"Well…" She paused again. "I assume he's black."

"Why? Because the rooster is black or because you think Deontay is a black name?"

Celeste didn't know what to say. She made a bit of a noise like she was about to form the first word of a sentence, then closed her mouth again.

"It's like those people who look like they dogs, isn't it?" Rory agreed with me.

"So how much is it that the fighting cock is worth?" Rosel jumped back in. "This can be from a very big range. So maybe a cock is brand new and no so good, so it is not worth no moneys. But also maybe a cock is a champion not only here in this small village, but also in Cusco or even Lima. Then it can be worth an amazing amounts.

Here in Peru what do you think is the salary for a working man? So maybe like one of our porter? It is only about eight hundred to one thousand a month, and remember my friends this is soles and not dollars."

That broke down to somewhere around 250 to 350 dollars per month.

"And how much is worth a champion fighting cock in a

small village like we are in now? The prizes for a pollon, a tournament, can be anywhere from starting at 1,000 soles, yes my friends a full-month salary for a working mans, and could even be so much as thirty-thousand soles which is more then many man make in even two years of hard work.

So you see that there is great money in this sport, and also because of this, there is great care for the animal. This rooster who look like you American boxing champion Deontay Wilder is receiving regular medical attention, daily training, and the best of foods.

So, we will continue our walk and maybe it is three kilometers only, more or minus, then we will come to the coffee farm where we will learn some things about how it is that the coffee is made and have our lunch. Vamanos my friends!"

We walked on. Beth walked slowly, which was totally fine. Rosel and I stayed with her and I did not at all mind the pace.

The group, lead by Raul, was about fifty yards ahead of us when they exited the village, rounded the corner, and disappeared into the jungle.

When we came to that same point, a full minute later, a local woman came running after Rosel. We stopped as they talked for a moment in Quechua. I obviously had no idea about what.

"Ok, just one moment my friends. You may walk ahead and I will catch right up."

So Beth and I walked on. It was only a three kilometer walk on a nice Peruvian flat path in the shade.

"I wouldn't have pegged you for a mortgage processer," I told her.

"Yeah, me neither."

"So, what does that even mean?"

"Well, when someone applies for a mortgage I have to go through all their documents, input them into the computer, make calls to their employers, that sort of thing."

"So a desk?"

"Cubicle."

"Hmmm."

"Yeah."

"Well, if you like it."

"I don't." We stopped so she could have some more water. "When I graduated my uncle knew a guy who owned a mortgage company so…" We started walking again. "My family all tells me it's a good job."

"I don't know what that means."

"I don't either!" She laughed.

"If you don't like it, and you spend most of your time there, then what's so good about it?"

She shook her head. "I don't know. I guess they mean the pay."

"Is your time for sale?" She just looked at me. "All of ours is, to a degree. But we have to decide how much we're willing to sell it for, and what we're willing to trade it for or not willing to trade it for."

She nodded and we kept placing one foot in front of the other. She thought it over, then spoke. "I live in Colorado. I've been thinking about being a white-water river guide in the summer and a ski instructor in the winter."

"Sounds great."

"But where does that lead?"

"Where does anything lead? Life is to be lived, not planned for."

"Yeah. I don't know. I think you're right but it's hard to think that way, you know? I mean all of our lives we've been taught the opposite."

Rosel came jogging up to us. He was a 5'6" man, weighed about 130 lbs, carrying a fifty-five-pound backpack and now, in his right hand, he carried a propane tank. Sweat dripped from his forehead.

"What is this?" I pointed to the propane tank.

"Propane."

"Well yeah, I can see that."

"One of the porters forgets it. So I will bring to lunch."

He put it down and rested for a moment. It was the first time I had seen him noticeably tired.

"Let me see that thing." I picked it up. "Holy shit." It was heavy. I would later Google it and find out that propane tanks weigh thirty-seven pounds. I put it back down.

"Ok, we walk."

"Well, let me get a hand on that thing." I reached down and grabbed one of the handles with my left hand. He grabbed a handle with his right.

"Thank you, my friend. You are the man." It was much easier to carry between the two of us than it was it would be for a single person.

So we walked. Every hundred yards or so we stopped and switched sides.

Twenty minutes later we came to the foot of a hill and saw the coffee farm, our rest spot and lunch break, ahead of us. We put the propane down and had some water.

"How you feeling?" I asked Beth.

"Fifty percent." She drank. "How about you?"

I felt fine, just fine. I wasn't looking forward to carrying two packs and half a propane tank up the hill, but it was what it was.

But then it wasn't. Rory saw us carrying the propane tank and he ran down to us.

"Bloody hell, you two legging this thing the whole way then?" I nodded. "Well give it here."

Rory shouldered the propane tank and we made our way to lunch.

****

"Ok super hikers! So what is the number one country for produce of coffee?"

"Um, I think it's Brazil mate." Liam said honestly.

"Maybe yes, and maybe no. Brazil make the most coffee, it is true. But how to measure what is number one? I think maybe it is not who make the most coffee but who make the best coffee. And Peru makes the best coffee, this is without debate."

Somehow I guessed there might be a tour guide in Brazil who would dare to debate this, but I let it go.

"So how are we making the coffee? In Peru, there is an adorable animal that look like the racoon. We are calling this animal the coati or uchunari. Besides being cute, these animals, like all animals, does what? In the mornings it makes its poop.

This coati poop is especially sought after, as it is the key to making Peruvian poop coffee."

"What? Yuk!" One of the girls from Alabama made a face.

"It is true. All over the world the best coffee is coming from poops. In most place they use the monkey, but here we have the very best coffee because we have the coati. The very best producers in Peru have turned to coatis in order to make this unique type of coffees. When coffee cherries are ripen and turn red they attract a variety of wild animals. Amongst them is this small, long-nosed relative of the racoon. So it sees the coffee cherry, eats of them, and then it does its poop.

The coffee bean is unable to be fully digest by the coatis, so the coffee cherry is only partially broken down by the, how you say?

"Stomach."

"Acids."

"Enzymes."

"Yes, then the nature happens. Workers collect the coati's nature, carefully wash and dry this product, then mill it to extract the bean, which is then roasted."

I made a mental note not to shake hands with any of the people who worked here. But they weren't around to shake hands anyway, they were in the back preparing our lunch.

"Once this process is complete, all that remain is the beautiful scent coffee beans, ready for consumption! This Peru coffee have no of bitterness, yet is still full-bodied and even sometime with taste of various jungle fruits.

This coffee is definitely expensive and sell for about twenty and even up to sixty American dollar per kilogram. You can find it in specialty coffee shops here in the Cusco region, or we can be buying some here from this very coffee farm, fresh and for discount."

"Anyone else fancy a cup of proper English tea with their lunch today then?" Rory asked and found plenty of takers. "These colonists with their coffee. Might as well get out of bed and just stick your nose right up a raccoon's ass, isn't that right Liam?"

After lunch, which included a nice steaming pot of fresh raccoon poop coffee, I returned for the toilet.

"How is it?" Ed asked me, inquiring about the toilet.

"I mean, you wouldn't like it if we were back in America, but…"

"How bad?"

"No, it's not bad. It's clean enough. I just don't understand why they don't have toilet seats. And why there's never any toilet paper."

"Because then it wouldn't be authentic?" Celeste rolled her eyes at me.

"Authentic. What are you playing at? Nothing we're doing here is authentic."

"Speak for yourself."

"We're on the same tour. Tour! We have porters running ahead of us with our tents and sleeping bags, somebody just made lunch for you and cleared away the plates, tonight we're stopping in a campsite that will have a fridge fully supplied with beers…"

"Bloody well hope so."

"…and you're wearing headphones half the time when you walk."

"Yeah, but I'm listening to the sounds of nature?" Celeste again rolled her eyes at me, then she walked away.

Ed eyed Abe's plate. Next to it sat his napkin. "You going to use that napkin?"

Abe looked at it. The social-justice warrior loved to preach about America hording resources and how much better off the world would be if nobody owned anything. But now, now that actual resources, like toilet paper, were in short supply and high demand, now he was starting to come around to the concept of ownership. A quick glance at him told the full story. He did not need to use the toilet right now. He did not immediately need the napkin. But maybe he would need it later on? Maybe it would be best if he hoarded the napkin for himself?

"You might not want it," Abe said meekly. "I think I wiped my mouth on it earlier."

"I'll take it," Ed said boldly.

"Well…"

"Half a Snickers bar once we're back on the trail."

"Deal."

Abe handed over his napkin.

"So, this afternoon, I think maybe it is a little more hill than this morning." Rosel told me.

"Ok."

"You are still strong?"

"I'm just fine."

"And Miss Beth?"

"Let's just keep walking," she told him.

"Good. So I think little by little, slowly, and we will get there. I am going to have Raul not to wait for us, and maybe we come into camp later than the others but this is ok. I will stay with you and we will go at whatever pace you wish."

Beth nodded and everyone got to walking.

Before the other group parted from us I caught up to Clint. "Hey, you have a headtorch?"

"Yeah."

"Mind if I borrow it? We might get into camp a few hours after you, could still be walking in the dark."

He didn't mind at all and fished it out of his bag for me.

****

"So here we have the natural growing avocado. If you look

up in the tree it look like the back of a bull!"

Beth and I stopped and had some water. She was doing great. One foot in front of the other, keeping a slow but steady pace.

"The original word of avocado comes from the Aztec words and it is the same as testicle."

Looking at the avocado tree they did look like a bunch of swinging balls. Still tasted good though.

"Have you always lived in the mountains?" I asked as we began our walk again.

"Yes. I grow up in a small village lik e the ones you have seen this week. And always hiking. When I was young, how is it to go to school? So to get to the school there is a path. In the morning it take one hour and forty-five minute to get down the hill to the school. Then after, hiking uphill, it take maybe two hour and fifteen minute to get home."

Rosel was the only guy I knew who could actually say, 'when I was your age I hiked two hours to school, both ways, in the mountains!' and be telling the truth.

This section of the original Inca Trail was mostly stone, about the width of an American sidewalk and cut through the tropical forest. It was up, then up some more, but the altitude wasn't bad and it was a nice hike.

"So, you haven't spoken much about Hiram Bingham," I said to Rosel after a few kilometers of silence.

"And what would I say? That he is the man that discover Machu Picchu? How can a man discover what another man has already build? And when Bingham come to Machu Picchu, what is there? Three families that live there all year and make their crops there. So he has discover another man's home? This is like me buying a plane ticket to America and discover your house. Then I rob it, take you valuable, and return to Peru with them. You want them back of course, but the museum tells you that this is not possible because you are not fit to take care of them. To this day only ten percent of the valuable that Hiram Bingham steals is returned to Peru. Just ten percent. So I do not think that this is a great man."

We walked on, staying at Beth's pace, which was slow but still steady. She was not going to give up.

"You have seen the Indiana Jones?" Rosel asked me. Then he hummed a bit of the score.

"Of course."

"I think this man is based of Hiram Bigham. He does no do any real science, he mess up everything everywhere that he go, he do not carry his own pack. The guide and porter around him they do what? They die and he does not care. Then he rob a grave, destroy a site, make a few more mistake, but he take a picture and look good so he can go home and look like a hero. Maybe this is Bingham? He discover Machu Picchu. How? By hiring guide and porter to lead him to Machu Picchu like they are no also men?"

I was beginning to be sorry I asked.

"No, I do no speak much about Hiram Bingham."

****

About five kilometers after lunch we had ascended the final hill for the day. I was quite sweaty due to having a pack on both my back and my front, but other than that I felt good. Raul had kept the main group fairly slow, giving them a real tour and allowing them to take pictures. The end result was we were only about fifteen minutes behind them.

We came to a rest area on the top of the mountain.

"We will rest here for maybe thirty minute, more or minus. Would you like the oxygen Miss Beth?" She shook her head no.

Rosel took out his finger device to read her oxygen levels and pulse. He looked at it. "No so bad. It is below good, but you are doing a little better. I think maybe I will bring the oxygen out and maybe you are change you mind. It will not hurt you."

He got out the oxygen tank and mask for her.

"And how about you Mr. Joel?"

"I'm fine."

"Yes, but you carry two pack and also with me the propane."

"So did you. And your one pack weighs as much as my two."

"Yes, but I do this every week. I think maybe you would no tell me if you is no fine."

"I wouldn't. But I am fine."

He motioned for me to hold out my hand. I did and he put the oxygen and pulse reader on it.

"So?"

He shrugged, "You are like Inca my friend."

The highlight of this rest area was an infinity swing. It started on solid earth of course, then you swung yourself off the edge of the world and, ideally, back again. We all had to have a turn.

There was nothing inherently scary about the swing. I was ninety-nine-point-nine percent sure that I would not fall off, so in reality there was nothing to be scared of. I was sure that it would have the illusion of being quite scary though, swinging off of the cliff. What honestly worried me was the swing's construction. At the end of the day it was nothing more than a couple of poles that two totally untrained men had driven into the ground. Believe me, there was no city inspector coming up here to check on their work or to renew their certificate for the 2019 season. It was very much swing at your own risk.

We did. It was fantastic. I had missed the experience of swimming in Humantay Lake, but I would not miss this. Off the edge of the world I went, clinging, literally, for dear life. The views were phenomenal, but I couldn't help myself from making stupid noises every time I swung forward. "Oh. Ok. Holy.... Oh boy. Ah..."

"Hope I don't die." Beth said as she climbed on the swing after me for her turn.

"Well, if you do, I'm going to throw your pack over the side."

"Fair."

****

Back on the trail we hiked on. We were at the top now and the trail gently went up and down. The altitude was only around nine-thousand feet. Beth was doing just fine, in fact, without the uphills, she was doing pretty well. The main group walked without the three of us, but they never really left my sight.

Ludwig must be going crazy, I thought to myself. Poor guy might have to stop and actually learn something.

"You know of in you country what is call The Pony Express?"

"Yeah, sure."

"This idea was invent here in the Andes mountain, by the Inca. How fast do you think it is that I can move on this trails if I do no have a pack?"

"I don't know. Pretty fast."

"Yes. Now imagine that I know that I only have to go maybe ten kilometers only, and after that I will have food and rest. So I can just go."

"Even faster than the two trail running couples, or Beth here when she's well."

"Perhaps it is not so in you country," he said, not wanting to be insulting. "But here in the mountain, yes, if I wish to disappear none but another Inca can keep up with me. So hundreds of years ago we have a system for deliver of the messages. Every ten to twenty kilometer there is a new man waiting for a message. When a important person from Cusco need a message deliver to Machu Picchu, or to someplace else, he give it to a runner who takes it very fast to the next man, and so on all of the way down the line. So you see the message is always move fast and never with rest. In this way the mail was move all throughout the entire Inca Empire."

We walked some more. A small butterfly joined us.

"So how big is the Incan Empire? It is even bigger than the Roman Empire. This is true. So how does the Spanish come here and defeat the Inca? Yes it is modern weapon and warfare, but mostly they bring with them what? The disease. These disease of you in Europe..."

"I'm not from Europe."

"Maybe not you my friend, but these disease of the white peoples are not the same as what we have here, and it kill many more people than the warfare ever does. Also, with much time, there is intermarriage or maybe is just rape, but many of the Inca people become Spanish and many of the Spanish peoples become Inca you see? Even I myself am twenty-five percent of the Spanish."

I nodded. "Similar stories all over the world."

"Yes. But always the Inca fight. We take to the hills to fight a different kind of war, and over much time. How do you call this, I think it is monkey warfare?"

I laughed a little, he wasn't sure why. "Sorry, that's just funny in English. You speak very well. Guerrilla warfare."

"Gorilla is what?"

"It's a large monkey, but..."

"This is what I say, monkey warfare."

"Yeah, I'm quite sure the saying is guerrilla warfare."

"But no monkey?"

"Definitely not."

"It is strange you language."

"Yeah."

"So we fight the war of the gorilla and in time, much time, what happen? The Spanish go home and Peru is form. Our own country again. So I think maybe the Inca were no conquered."

****

"Lovely hikers!" The three of us had caught up to Raul and his group. They were moving slowly, taking photos, on a real tour, and Beth had done a great job of keeping up a slow but steady walk. Rosel addressed the entire group now. "Here we all gather as a family so we can go around the corner and see what? I think it will be your first look at Machu Picchu with you own eyes."

We clapped.

"So we will come to our campsite for the night, high in the mountain, we will have a look across the valleys and there, very small, on another mountain we will see the Machu Picchu! Vamanos!"

We rounded the corner and came to our campsite. It was an amazing place, a large flat area roughly the size of a football field, on the side of our mountain. The porters had all of our tents set up. There was a permanent lodge and I could smell dinner cooking, llamas grazed in the distance.

Way across the valley, beyond the river, and high up in the next mountain was a small brown speck. Damn I need to get Lasik, I thought to myself.

That was alright though. Everyone was really excited about getting their first glance at Machu Picchu. If I'm being totally honest, at that moment I was just really excited to sit down and open my can of Pringles.

After dinner I finally found a free moment to talk to the girl from Alabama who had come into our tent early this morning to cuddle with Clint.

"Do you have your own tent again?"

"Yeah, they're all two-person tents so I've always kind of been the odd woman out."

"That is seriously not fair." She looked at me, unsure how to respond. "If you ever want to rotate with one of us unlucky mortals I'd love my own tent." Again she looked confused. "Truth is I'm getting really sick of Clint." Her mouth moved a little bit but she did not speak. "Yeah he's always hogging the covers, plus we're constantly arguing about who gets to be the big spoon." She tilted her head like a dog trying to understand English. "So if you think you can stand sharing a tent with him you sure would be doing me a favor, I'd love to get rid of the guy."

"I think he's a pretty nice guy." She said. So far so good. "I don't know why you wouldn't like him! Seems like he's always been nice to you!"

She looked angry and walked away. Now it was my turn to sit there with a dumb look on my face. Did she not understand the very simple code that I was laying out? I may as well have just come up to her and handed her a note: "Do you want to spend the night alone with Clint in a private tent? Check yes, no, or maybe."

"How'd it go?" Clint asked a few minutes later.

"Um. I don't know."

In the evening, after dinner, I made my way to the toilet. The building was down a set of ten or so Inca stairs, big stairs.

My body had stiffened up during dinner. I swung one leg around, unable to bend it at the knee, threw it over the side, then crashed down on it. No knee bend to absorb impact, no ankle to gently roll, just a lumbering Frankenstein-like goon trying to descend huge stone steps. Next I threw my right leg forward and crashed down on it, eighteen inches closer to the toilet. In this fashion I made my way to the bottom and joined the line.

"Let me ask you something," I said to the three people at the bottom of the stairs, all from another tour. "The average Inca man is what, five foot five?"

"They're short."

"And people get taller every generation. So six-hundred years ago when they were building these trails they couldn't have been any taller than five feet, maybe even less."

"Yeah."

"So why would a bunch of five-foot-tall men build the largest damned steps I've ever been on?"

"You know that's a really good point."

We stood for a moment, watching two Asian girls, both stiff as a board, try to make their way down the stairs and join the line for the toilet.

In time I heard a flush, then two more, and then I was up. I went in and closed the door. I was in pitch black.

Where the hell is the light switch? As my eyes slowly adjusted and I put my face six inches from the wall, I came to the conclusion that there was no light switch. I stepped back outside.

A Canadian guy stepped forward to go next.

"Hang on." I stopped him. "Borrow your headtorch?"

With the light of a Canadian headtorch I made my way back into the stall. No seat, no toilet paper.

On legs that had been hiking for the past ten hours, not to

mention days, I squatted above the toilet and hoped for the best. When I was done I used my dinner napkin as sparingly as I could prior to moving on to my ever-depleting personal stash of toilet paper.

"All you," I told the Canadian guy as I handed back his head-torch, sound of a flush still in the background.

As my stiff body came up the stairs I heard sounds of yelling in Quechua.

I made my way over to the porter's area and saw two of our porters brawling like a couple of miniature cowboys.

They were standing, both steadily on their feet, latched on to each other's sweaters, pushing back and forth and occasionally throwing a looping right hand. It looked like a peewee hockey fight minus the ice.

Clint joined me. "Should we do something?" He casually asked.

"I don't know. They're evenly matched, no weapons. Doesn't seem like any of my business." He stood silently for a moment, then shrugged. So we sat down.

"I think the older one's going to gas," Clint said to me.

The older guy, he may have been fifty, landed three or four real nice body blows before eating a head shot from his opponent. Then they both went back to pushing.

"Naw. Have you paid any attention the last few days? These guys don't gas."

"Care to make it interesting?"

"What do you have in mind?"

"Twenty."

"You're on."

We watched a while longer; the younger guy shoved the older porter into a tree and held him pinned there.

"You're betting on the old guy, right?" Clint asked me.

"Yep."

While my man was pinned to the tree I reached into my hiking pants and pulled out a Snickers bar. I opened it, broke it in half, and handed half to Clint.

"Thanks." We sat and enjoyed our snickers bars. "Oh! By the way!" Clint said excitedly. "You've got your own tent tonight!"

"Oh yeah?" Clint's porter landed a clean left hand, while still pinned against the tree. A small trickle of blood flowed from my guy's nose.

"Yeah. April, I think her name's April, she said that you mentioned that you and I are getting on each other's nerves..."

"I can't stand ya."

"Good. And that she could move to our tent if you were too much of a jerk for me to bunk with."

"And I am of course."

"Oh, big time. Major jerk."

"Nice."

We shook hands as the porters broke away from the tree and started to throw punches again.

"What do we have here then?" Rory joined us.

"Porter fight."

"Well fair play to them." He sat and joined us. I pulled the second Snickers from my pocket and handed it to him. He looked at me and nodded. "Cheers mate."

"We've got a twenty on it," Clint told him.

"Dollars or soles?"

"I don't know." Clint looked at me. "Are we betting dollars or soles?"

"Whatever you want."

They were shoving again. My porter spun and pinned the other guy up against the tree. Then he untangled his right hand and landed some more good body blows. Clint didn't like this.

"Soles," he said.

"I'd like to get in on this," Rory said. Then he stood up and called across camp. "Oy! Liam. Get over here mate, and bring some beers for the lads!"

When Rory yelled it got the attention of the other porters. They looked at us, looked at the guys who were fighting, said something in Quechua, and broke them up.

"Looks like that's that fellows," I said.

But that was not that. All the porters went inside of a tool shed, away from the eyes of the Gringos. A few seconds later the yelling started again and we heard men crashing into walls.

"Alright boys, all bets are off."

Clint and I agreed to this and moved on.

"Happy birthday dear Rosel, happy birthday to you!" We all cheered.

We were gathered up in the main lodge again. Somebody had bought a round of beers, our chef had baked a cake.

"Thank you my friends."

Abe stood up, and in a perfect Rosel impression said, "I think maybe this is a the good time to talk about birthday, no? It is 41 year and nine month that my parent, the Inca people, come together to make me, the greatest hiker in all of the worlds."

We all laughed, ate cake, and swigged beer.

"So I think, little by little, we will go around the circle and talk about how it is that I am the greatest guide in all of the county of all of the world. Please to go first my friend." Abe pointed at Rory.

"He's got the nicest calves, hasn't he Liam."

"Aye, aye. Good firm buttocks too."

"I'll second that!" The women from Colorado shouted and her husband shrugged.

"Nobody knows more about monkey shit!"

"Lots of knowledge, doesn't take up much space!"

"Got me hooked on cocaine tea!"

"Thank you my friends. Thank you. Forty-one years. I think maybe this is a good way to celebrate. I am with good peoples, nice hike, and tomorrow we will wake up to beautiful sunrise over the valleys. Thank you for making a good birthday. Cheers."

I crawled into my tent, my luxurious, single-occupancy,

tent. I took my boots off, threw my pack down, spread out on top of my bag, and heard the buzz of a mosquito in my ear.

When April, I think her name was April, took her stuff and switched so she could sleep in the tent with Clint tonight, she had forgotten to zip this tent back up.

"Son of a bitch," I mumbled to myself.

I grabbed my cell phone, turned on the light, and started hunting. There were three mosquitoes flying around in my restricted airspace. I'm an animal lover. Most people who say that are talking only about fur-bearing mammals, the cute ones. I'm fine with all animals. I'm not afraid of snakes, bees, don't have any problem with spiders. I don't step on ants when I'm outside. If they stay out of the house, they can do whatever they want outside. That's fair. When I find a random bug in the house, I gently trap him in some tissue paper then release him outside.

Mosquitoes are there to bite me and feed on my blood. The hell with them. I kill on site.

But there was the problem. It's not so easy to spot a mosquito when you're searching for it. One would move, buzz, I'd see it in the light for a second... Then it was gone. I'd find it in the light again, realize that I needed two hands to kill it, try to put the phone down, and ultimately lose it. So I had to then go back to hunting. I sat patiently, waiting to catch site of one again, then, slowly, I would put the phone in my mouth, clap my hands violently, and... empty.

I believe I hunted mosquitoes for a solid hour that night. Clint better be having a great time.

CHAPTER 7: AGUAS CALIENTES

"Lovely hikers." I heard Rosel's voice outside of my tent.

"No lovely hikers this morning. Just me."

I crawled out of my sleeping bag and unzipped the door. Rosel poked his head in. "I have room service for you." He handed me a metal mug of hot coca tea. If you have to wake up at five a.m. this was one of the best ways to do so, I thought to myself as I took my first hot sip. He looked around. "Where is Mr. Clint?"

"Mr. Clint found himself a girl."

Rosel smiled a big smile. "Ah, very good!" Then he offered me a high five. So I sat there, a grown man in skin-tight white Under Amour long johns, disheveled hair, drinking cocaine tea, five a.m. in the morning in the Andes mountains, high fiving an Incan. "I think the sun will come up very soon so we will go to the field and watch. Very good, muy bueno." He left for the next tent.

The entire group gathered at the side of the mountain waiting for the sun to rise. Dim light was available now and I watched wild llamas in the fog. We had done it, we had crossed the mountains and now we would finally see the sun over Machu Picchu. The birds started to chirp, the llamas and alpacas walked in and out of the fog, and Rory lead us in the Manchester United football club's fight song:

"I'm forever blowing bubbles,
Pretty bubbles in the air,
They fly so high,
They reach the sky,

And like my dreams they fade and die!
Fortunes always hiding,
I've looked everywhere,
I'm forever blowing bubbles,
Pretty bubbles in the air!
United!
United!

Come on lads! We did it! Up the mountain we went, right good effort! Everyone now:

When shadows creep..."

"Will you shut up!" The women from Colorado yelled. "Honestly it's like your mind is a hollow hole that constantly has to be filled with noise."

"Honey." Her husband tried to rein her in.

"No! No! He has ruined every beautiful moment of this trip with his nonstop nonsense! Just look at the view you dumb chimpanzee!"

Everyone stopped. Rory looked genuinely hurt.

"Well go on then."

"What?"

"Have a go. I'm an easy target. Talk too much, don't know when to keep me big mouth shut."

"Rory..."

"Not much to look at. Ugly, don't mind saying it. Bald. Got no kids, not much money, haven't much to offer. But I've a big heart, don't I Liam?'

"You do mate."

"Always the first round on me at the pub. Never left a man behind, never said a bad word about anyone that I wouldn't say right to 'em. Just want everyone to have a good time, have a bit of a laugh. Didn't mean nothing by it."

"Rory..."

But Rory got up and walked away from the group.

****

The morning hike was easy on the lungs but tough on the knees. For two hours we went down sharply, leaning heavily into our hiking poles to take some of the weight off of our joints.

Beth proclaimed that she was better this morning and could carry her own pack.

"If I were you, I'd still let me carry it," I told her. Then I thought it through and corrected myself, telling her more honestly, "Well, no, I wouldn't. But someone smarter than me would."

She was not smarter than me, she was just as stubborn. She was feeling a bit better and would carry her own pack today. It may not have been the doctor-recommended move, but it is exactly what I would have done. Meanwhile, Abe would still be riding a mule if the option existed.

I would have carried her pack, but the truth was I was glad not to. These downhills were tearing my joints up. I didn't feel like an Inca today; I felt like an old man going in for a double knee replacement.

I leaned hard on my hiking poles and kept descending.

"Lovely hikers! Here we see the hidroelectrica station this is generate all of the power for the city of Cusco and also for the other city of the area. As you can see there is a great waterfall, of three hundred meter and maybe even a little more. This power is harnened, har... How you say?"

"Harnessed."

"Yes, thank you. This power is harnesseded and convert into much energies. So you see, even today the Urubamba River is giving life to the Inca peoples."

In the afternoon we started a long flat walk along the railroad tracks.

"You will no need you walking sticks anymore," Rosel told us.

"Yeah, yeah, I've bloody heard that before," Rory grumbled as we all handed over our walking sticks to the porters. "Hundred quid says we'll be sweating up the side of a mountain within the hour."

But the walk was flat. Follow the railroad tracks for three hours, more or minus, and we would be in Aguas Calientes, hot water, the city at the base of Machu Picchu. It was the last little bit of our hike. At the end we would have a shower, a meal in a restaurant, and a visit to the hot springs.

For the first time on our journey the path was crowded. Really crowded. We had seen other groups on the trail, usually running into one or two other tours per day, and generally sharing our campsites with them, but for the most part the sixteen of us and our guides had been totally alone. Now I felt like I was walking in downtown Chicago.

They took the trains here by the hundreds. Brought in luxury from Cusco then dropped off a mere three-hour flat walk from Aguas Calientes, all so they could tell all their friends back home that they had "hiked" to Machu Picchu.

"Did you know that this is the road that Hiram Bingham took when he discovered Macho Picknew?" one girl said to her friend. They both wore designer hiking ensembles free of dirt, sweat, or odors.

"Really?" the other one squealed. "We're like, walking on history."

I was angry at them; they hadn't earned it. The did not make their own way over the mountains like we had.

Just then two of our porters ran by us, literally ran. They had fifty-five pounds on their backs, sweat was dripping in huge pools below them.

Ok, maybe we didn't exactly make our own way here either. But at least we didn't take the train.

Clint was walking with Liam and Rory about fifty feet in front of me. I caught up and fell in with them.

"What's up fellows?"

"My bloody knee is killing me mate."

I nodded. There was nothing else to be said or done so I turned the conversation to Clint. "Hey, how'd it go last night?"

"Yeah, fine."

"Yeah fine?"

"I know how it went." Liam said with a small laugh. "We had the tent right next to them, didn't we Liam?"

"Could hear everything."

"Oh yeah?"

"Your man Clint was up all night having a cuddle."

"Alright," Clint said in an annoyed tone.

"Kept us up late with a long conversation about Jesus."

"How was that?" I asked.

"I'll be rooming with you again tonight, that's for sure."

I walked with Ed, Abe, and Celeste. We covered a kilometer in silence.

"It was a beautiful hike," Abe said.

We all sort of nodded and walked a bit more in silence. Then Ed dropped the bomb on us. "I have cancer."

We all turned. Celeste stopped. "Is it…"

"Terminal? Yep."

Celeste covered her mouth. Then, eyes wet, she hugged Ed.

"Come on now…" He didn't know what to say or do. "Ok, ok."

"But what about chemo?"

"It's too far. That's ok. I got to see a lot of the world in my day, had some good people around me. Glad I got to take this hike while I still can."

"How long do you have?" I asked and Celeste shot me a look. "What?" I shrugged my shoulders.

"Oh hell, doctors. What do they know? One says months, another says it may be five years? Come on, we'll never get to Machu Picchu if we're just standing around."

So we walked again.

"It's not a bad thing though." Ed went on. "To know that

your own clock is ticking. Makes you see things differently; appreciate things you may have overwise skipped. I've done a few things right; have other things I wish I could do over. Gives me a chance to think about it and even do what I can to correct some of my mistakes."

"Yeah."

"Of course, if I'm being honest, I'd rather just be twenty-five again and splitting a bottle of Jack with the guys in the barracks."

An hour later Abe and I were walking alone when we overtook Rory.

He was limping badly. He had an old T-shirt tied around his knee as a brace and he had picked up a big stick to lean on.

"You ok?" Abe blurted out.

"Bloody stupid question mate. Me knee is shot; I'll tell you that much."

"Think you can make it?"

"Can't just lay down and die here now, can I?"

"Let me carry your bag," I told him.

"Looking for another handjob then, are you Joel? I told you, nobody carries my kit."

"Who gave you a handjob?" Abe asked me.

"Nobody."

"Did Rory...?"

Rory and I both stopped walking and stared at him. "No!"

"Bloody hell." Rory shook his head and continued to stare at him. "Beth mate."

"Beth gave you a han..."

"Nobody gave me a handjob!"

We walked in silence for a bit. Rory limping along and Abe wondering who may have given me a handjob.

"Well go on then," Rory said to us. "You don't have to limp along with me."

"We're not leaving you. What kind of bullshit would that be?"

Some time passed and the three of us kept walking, or limping, along. Soon Liam came jogging back to us.

"Well look at you," Rory said to him. "All huffing and puffing, sweating like a fat man at the fryer."

"They said you was in trouble mate. Limping and such."

"And you come running back here, did you? Like you was me bloody wife?"

"I'm just your mate, aren't I?"

"Well how much further is it then?"

"Bout a kilometer, more or less. Let me take that." Liam, who had left his pack in Aguas Calientes, reached for Rory's pack.

"I told ya already, nobody carries me kit! So you can fuck off with that, the lot of you!"

"Alright, steady on," Liam said. Rory kept limping. "You going to slag me off if I at least walk with you?"

"Fall in."

So the four of us walked on at Rory's pace.

****

Aguas Calientes could only be described as a city in the clouds. It instantly reminded me of *Star Wars* and I wondered if Lando Calrissian might be running it.

The town was on a sharp hill, the lower part butting up to the Urabamba River, the top of the city disappeared into the sky. The streets were basically all cobblestone allies, narrow, almost exclusively for foot traffic. They were lined with small restaurants, markets selling sweaters and such, massage, pharmacy, an endless number of hostels, and pubs. This town was a staging point for Machu Picchu. In the morning the entire town would clear out and head up the mountain to one of the seven wonders of the modern world. A few hours later, the town would fill up completely with the next batch of Gringos. Like the tide going out then coming back in again, it was a one-night stop, every hotel, eatery, and watering hole always at full capacity.

It also had Wifi, meaning everyone was now glued to their

phone.

"Joel!"

"Hey mom," I said into my phone.

"I can't believe it!"

"How come you always sound surprised when I call. The caller ID says it's me."

"Yes, but you're in Peru!"

"Yeah. They have phone service here."

My dad jumps on the line. "How much does it cost per minute?"

"I'm not really sure."

"When we were in Italy, boy did they ever do a number on us! Julie, do you remember that?"

"Oh my goodness, yes! Joel, we got home and do you know what our phone bill was?"

"No idea."

"Well it was high. Your father had to get on the phone with ATT."

"I was arguing with them for hours."

"Joel, you have to be careful about making long distance calls from other countries." My mother warns me. I lower the phone a little bit and exhale.

"What kind of plan do you have?" My dad asks.

"Ten dollars a day. Only on the days when I turn my phone on."

"And you can talk all day?"

"Joel, you have to read the fine..." My mother starts but my dad interrupts her.

"Julie, I'm talking."

"Well can't I talk too? I'm the one who picked up the phone!"

"Joel." My dad continues. "Did you read the fine print?"

"No. How are things..."

"What a number they did to us when we got back from Italy! Julie, what was the phone bill?"

"I don't know, but it was high! Your father had to get on the phone with ATT."

"So you've said."

"He was on the phone with them for hours."

"Hours." My old man confirms.

"Ok, mom, dad! I didn't call from Peru to discuss how much it might or might not cost to call from Peru."

"You have to be careful with these phone companies."

"You have to read the fine print."

"So we've been hiking through the mountains. Altitude of up to fifteen thousand feet, steep climbs, up to twenty-four kilometers per day."

"You know your father's been working out too. He goes to Aqua Fit."

"Forty-five minutes in the pool. I've done it three times this week."

"So are we going to the hot springs?" one of the girls from Alabama asked cheerfully.

"I think maybe this is no for you."

"Why not?"

"Many persons every day, they come here and without a shower go to sit in the hot spring."

"Oh."

"Then also they make there their toilet and the water smells much of urine."

I had heard enough. I retreated to my hotel room.

Clint finished his shower while I made notes in my journal. When it was my turn I stood in the clean hot water for half an hour. I would likely have stood there longer if we didn't have dinner plans as a group.

****

"Aqui." I pointed at the menu. The translation read roast Guinea pig.

"Si?" the girl asked me. It was obviously something only the locals ever ordered, but I was here in Peru, why not try a

Guinea pig?

"Claro que si! Porque no?" I told her in my insanely accented Spanish. She nodded and took my order.

"Oh! You order the Guinea Pig!" Rosel said excitedly. "Very good my friend." He slapped me on the back.

Rosel then stood and tried to get the table's attention. "Ok my friends. I think it is all about tomorrow. We will see Machu Picchu."

We cheered.

"Lovely hikers, it is best to see early in the morning, before the crowds is so large. So I think maybe we meet in the lobby of you hotel at four o'clock in the morning. Is this ok?"

We all agreed, easily, that this was fine.

"In the morning maybe there is no so much to eat, so you must bring some water bottle and you own snack."

"How much walking is there tomorrow?"

"No so much, I think it is very little for you."

"Bullocks. I've bloody well heard that before, haven't I? You can just piss right off with it mate 'cause I don't believe you."

"Maybe there is fifty stairs."

"That means five hundred, doesn't it Liam? I know how you Peruvian lot counts."

"So tomorrow there will be no room service. Raul and I will not knock on you doors and bring coca tea, so I think you must be setting an alarm for youselves. It is ok, yes?"

Everyone nodded yes. I knew damned well I'd be sitting in the lobby at four a.m. pissed off that only half of our group was awake and there.

The eyes of a charred Guinea pig stared back at me, its mouth wide open, ugly teeth pointing everywhere. I had what was essentially an entire dead rat on my plate. I took a deep breath. *Ok, it's just not what you're used to, but it's no different than eating a chicken.* I grabbed a leg, claws and all, pulled it off, shut down my mind, and took a bite.

"Ok, guys, guys!" Celeste called to all of us. "Now that the guides are gone, we need to decide how much we're going to tip them. Should we give them 20 dollars each? Like if all of us chip in twenty dollars that's over three hundred dollars. That's good, right?"

"Twenty dollars? Are you having a laugh? The man's been keeping you alive for a week and you're going on about twenty bloody dollars."

"You have to have respect for the local economy."

"It's Tom love."

"Huh?"

"Tom tit." I chime in. "Cockney rhythming slang. It means shit. Twenty bucks is a shit tip."

"Aye, aye. What do you say Joel?"

"You guys can do whatever you want. I'm out. I'm giving him a hundred bucks."

"You are such an American," Celeste groans.

"Yep. So are you."

"No, I'm not!" she fires back in a fake English accent that she's pretending is real. "I'm a citizen of the world."

"Oh yeah? Let me see your passport. You know, the one that says America on it."

"My passport doesn't say 'America' on it. It says 'The United States of America'?"

"Well it doesn't say 'citizen of the world' on your passport, I can tell you that for sure. If you were a citizen of the world then you wouldn't need a thousand-dollar guided tour of the Andes, with catered food, bottled water, and two-hundred-dollar hiking boots. All brought to you in good old English."

"We happen to be in America right now! Peru is South America?"

"Yeah, 'cause kids around the globe who dream of coming to America one day, they're all really hoping to weave llama fur for nickels in Peru. That's what they're thinking about when they think of America."

"You giving him a hundred dollars then? Are you Joel?"

"Yeah."

"Good man. What do you say Liam? A hundred pound each then, that's worth a bit more than your American dollars, isn't it?" Rory grins. "I'm just having a laugh mate. Good lot you Americans. Shoved your muskets right up our bums twice, didn't they Liam? Gave it to us right good and proper, told us to fuck right off of their continent. You get it good up the old bum like that twice, all you can do is have a laugh."

"I'm in for a hundred quid."

"A bit of the old Queen's money, eh, sort the guides right out? Proper like."

"That's right. Good lot those two, Rosel and Raul, proper."

"Do you see what you've started?" Celeste glares at me, her fake English accent gone now.

"Yeah, other people at the table actually tipping two hard working men who took us across the mountains."

"I'm in for a hundred." Ed pulls out his wallet and the others start to do the same.

"This is how you Americans ruin economies. You start throwing around your money, but it's not sustainable. You just go around barking in English..."

"You're speaking in English..."

"...and the next thing you know you have ruined everything authentic about yet another country."

"I have? You're wearing a llama fur sweater with Machu Picchu sewed into it and a leather cowboy hat. Yeah, you look authentic."

"When I go someplace I assimilate? It's called respect for the native country." She glances at my plate, which now just contains a charred head of a Guinea pig. "OMG, I cannot believe you ate that thing." She puts her hands up in front of her mouth and turns her face away. "Disgusting."

"My friends." Rosel shook his head. "My friends, you are very kind." Celeste crossed her arms and looked angry.

"Hell of a guide. Isn't that right lads?" We all cheered. "Three cheers for Rosel. Hip hip!"

"Hooray!"

"Hip hip!"

"Hooray!

"Hip hip!"

"Hooray."

"Thank you. Thank you, my friends, my family of hikers this week. It has been my honor to lead you on this tour and I hope, truly, that you have enjoy."

We clapped for him again.

"So tomorrow we will see Machu Picchu!"

More clapping.

"Remember again, we will leave in the morning, very early. This way we can be the first people there, we will see the sunrise, and maybe even for a short period of time we will have the entire place just to our self and only a small number of others before the big crowd show up. So Raul and I will not wake you up tomorrow. There is no coca tea room service."

We all laughed.

"As we have plan, we all meet on our own in the lobby of you hotel at four in the a.m. Is it ok if we do this?"

We all quickly agreed again. Four am was early, but this is why we were here. It was worth it.

"Thank you again my friends. We will see you in the early mornings." He waved and exited.

"Right good chap."

"Proper."

We all sat silently for a moment, then Rory asked the group, "Anyone else fancy a pint?"

****

After dinner I went straight to bed. It was close to ten p.m. already and my alarm was set for 3:45 a.m.

Clint came in around 2 a.m. I know this because I woke to the sounds of him puking.

"You alright in there dude?"

"Ahhhh…"

He puked again.

Then I heard the light thump of a toilet seat falling on his head. The toilet seats in Peru, when the toilet actually has a seat, absolutely never stay up. This is normally a problem for me because I either have to hold the seat up with one hand while I pee, or I end up pissing on the seat after it falls. Since I haven't had my head inside of a toilet since college, it just now occurred to me that the seat would also fall on the back of your noggin while puking.

I rolled over and went back to sleep.

Thirty minutes later I woke to a thunderous noise that shook the very foundations of the hotel. It was Clint, blowing his dinner out the back door. I couldn't imagine what the bathroom would look like when I would have to go in there in an hour. Didn't want to. I rolled over and went back to sleep.

"Judy."

I half woke again. I may have mumbled the word "huh?".

"Ohhhh!"

I was three quarters awake now, confused as to where I was and what the hell was going on.

"Ahhhh!"

Now I had it figured out. I was awake in a hotel room, in Peru, listening to a fully-grown drunk jerking himself off in a bed that was roughly a foot away from my bed.

CHAPTER 8:
MACHU PICCHU

At 3:45 my alarm went off. I sat up, head in my hands, and took a two-minute break sitting on the side of my bed. My snooze alarm went off, indicating that I had actually been sitting there for ten minutes.

Dim lights in the room showed Clint, thankfully with his pants pulled back up, sound asleep in his hiking boots.

I pulled on my own shoes and got to the lobby at 3:59 a.m.

At 4:45 a.m. I sat in the lobby, annoyed, still waiting for half of our group to show up. Ludwig wanted to go now and leave them all asleep in their damned beds. Frankly, I agreed with him.

We took the bus up the steep hill. There were one or two die hard hikers who had started off at 3 in the morning and would reach the top, in a sweaty mess, by sunrise. But ninety-nine percent of the crowd was done with their hike, the busses took us to the peak.

There was a crowd there, and a line, but I imagined it would be much worse in a few more hours.

"Bloody hell," Rory grumbled as we marched up step after step.

"It is maybe only five, maybe ten minute, of step to the top." Rosel told him. "No so much."

"I've heard that before. 'Rory, you don't need you sticks. Rory, it is very flat. Rory, it is no so far now.' You're a bloody lying little twat and if I could catch you I'd hold you up by your ankles and shake you till that tip I gave you fell out. Bloody stairs. If you Incas were so advanced you would have invented a lift."

****

And then we were there. I had seen it many times on TV, seen all the photos, but we were standing there looking at Machu Picchu.

We may not have been the very first group, but honestly, we were early enough. Hardly any other people were there. Alpacas grazed freely. The soft glow of the sun, still behind the mountains, gave everything that perfect Hollywood hue. I pulled out my phone and took the picture you see on the cover of this book.

"My friends. Welcome you all to Machu Picchu! Please, sit here and have a nice look. Just for you, and we will have maybe ten minutes of silence."

Rory held up his hands. Even he would not speak.

We were here. We were not a group of *someday* type of people. We were *today* kinds of people. I was at Machu Picchu today. If you're reading this book then I hope you are on a plane right now. I hope you are a today sort of person too.

"So what is the Machu Picchu? First in the Quechua language it mean Old Mountain. But what does the Machu Picchu build for? Some say it was for the guarding and protection of Inca Empire. Some say it is the palace of the Inca, the great chief of all the peoples, others say it was only his vacation house. How you say? His summer home.

How does it come to be? Some crazy people will tell you that it was build with the help of alien. I do no think so. This is only talk of people who do no wish to recognize the intelligence and advanced works of the Inca. Just like the fool and grave robber Hiram Bingham, I will no talk about alien."

Clint sank further and further down as Rosel continued to speak. He nodded forward then shook himself back to life.

"...is what is called The Guardhouse. As you can see it sits high over the Machu Picchu and has a good views all around. This is where the Inca soldiers would be and they would be watching the Sun Gate and the Inca Trail beyond, and also have a view to watch the west entrance and the main Inca Trail from Vilcabamba."

Finally, Clint's head flopped forward and he began to snore. Loudly.

"So how many peoples lived at the Machu Picchu? It is estimate that the city would have maybe seven hundred or so peoples at any one time. Most would be servant, farmer, and workers of course."

One of the girls from Alabama raised her hand.

"Yes, you have question?"

"Where is the bathroom?"

"Ah, very good question. Later I will show you where the Inca made his toilet. The chief's bathroom is very well preserve."

"No, um, I meant for me."

"Oh, this was outside the gates."

"Ok, um, how do I get there?"

"No, this is no now possible. Once you are inside of the Machu Picchu you can no go out and come back in. If you go out, you are out."

"What?"

"Yes. Otherwise you must buy a whole new ticket to enter and it is maybe fifty dollar of American money. This is if there are any ticket left for today, which maybe yes and maybe no."

"So, wait... What? I just need to..." She looked aghast. "How much longer is the tour?"

"Maybe three more hour, more or minus. You will see behind me a large field where the people of Machu Picchu is growing they corn, maze, and what? Of course the potato."

"Here we have what is referrer to as the Inca Bridge."

About a ten-minute hike away from the main site we now stood looking at an extremely narrow and sketchy bridge that connected two extremely narrow and sketchy-looking parts of an original Inca trail leading to Machu Picchu.

"There is a much talk about the Inca Trail, as if there is only one. The Inca have thousands of kilometers of trail, including the Inca trail which we journey to get to Machu Picchu this week. What you are looking at here my friends is an original piece of one of the many of the trail. It is now close as it is very dangerous."

The trail disappeared into the mountains. It couldn't have been more than two feet wide, and maybe only twelve to eighteen inches in some parts, no walls, no way to catch yourself, and nothing but death if you stumbled.

"Do you think maybe the Incas were crazy?" Rosel asked us and we nodded. "Maybe yes, and maybe no. Maybe the Inca is less afraid of the heights than other race, and maybe also with better balance in the mountain."

"You ever hiked that section?" Abe asked him.

"Yes. I was very scared."

"So these womens are the most beautiful of the Inca girls and they are recruit to live here and serve the Inca. And what is this structure called? It is the Temple of the Virgins."

"I'd solve that problem right quick, wouldn't I Liam?"

"Aye, aye."

"Ah, but maybe there is very strict capital punishment for those who anger the Inca? So let us talk, brief, about the Inca law and what happen when you break. Penalty could be personal or collective for you entire village even, accord to the crime. Since the purpose of Inca law was to teach a lesson to the offender and prevent re-occurrence by any member of the village, both mutilation and death penalty were used in regular life. For minor crime, maybe you get a public scolding."

"Don't care," Rory said. "Had it before. Me mum's always yelling at me in public, isn't she Liam? Don't matter how old I get."

"She's a good mum to you."

"Aye, the best."

"Yes, but maybe some crime is more serious? So what happen for theft? The Inca will do mutilation."

"Never stole nothing, never will. Got me problems, but I'm honest. No man will say I'm not."

"And what about for serious crime such as homicide? Then it is death."

"Wouldn't hurt a fly if he didn't deserve it. Not so bad this Inca law."

"Yes, and also consider serious, also punish by death, is both adultery and second offense of drunk."

These two caught Rory's attention.

"If you is drunk twice, or you have the sex with a women who is no you wife, then you will be stone or push off the cliff."

Rory was silent. Evidently the Incan laws were no longer in his favor.

"Few peoples had access to this place, that is call The Temple of the Sun, since that the ceremonies for the ordinary people were made on the public square, only the priest and the Inca, the chief, could enter to the Temple of the Sun."

In the back the girl from Alabama danced in circles and squeezed her legs together. She looked like she was going to cry.

"This is a semi-circle construction built over a strong rock, adapt to the natural environment. Do you know that Machu Picchu has survive many earthquake yet still stand? Why? Even though they build with stone and no mortar, the Inca peoples is very superior builders.

So here, the Temple of the Sun, there's a tower with a trapezoidal window, built over a rock of pure granite. In this place the persons who were in charge of the religion, the worship of Inti, the god of the sun, they keep several mummies to be worship. These mummies places are called the royal tombs. The mummies is an important part of the religion to the sun."

We hiked up stairs to the highest place in the old village, the Inca citadel, a beautiful view of the entire layout of Machu

Picchu.

"And finally my friends, I wish to show of you the Intihua-tana, the Inca sundial. This is the most important of all Machu Picchu.

The Inca believe this stone hold the sun in its place along its journey in the sky. It is build with exact precise. At midday on the equinoxes the sun stand exactly above the pillar, and cast no shadow at all. On June twenty one, the stone is casting the longest shadow on its southern side and on December twenty one, a much shortest one on its northern side.

Looking closely at the Intihuatana you will see many little step and other dent. The purpose of this is no known for sure, but I think they likely serve astronomical purposes, while others were most likely of ceremonial, perhaps for the placement of sacrifice or mummies of holy ancestors.

One myth say that the Inca believed that tying the sun to stones like these on key dates prevented her from going down for good. For the Inca know, that if the sun goes out, all life come to an end."

"So please my friends. Now you may take some time for you own, have a walk, have a picture, and thank you so much for coming to our beautiful country of Peru and to learn some of the Inca peoples."

Rosel shook hands and accepted hugs all around, then, just as he had stepped into our lives, he was gone. Forever a memory, a part of our wonderful journey to Machu Picchu.

We stood there, awkwardly, a group of sixteen hikers who were no longer a group. In seconds I would walk one way, Celeste and Abe another. Ed would go his own way, Rory and Liam theirs. The trail runners would all run off, the Alabama girls to the bath-room, Silent Roberta to the left, Clint to the right. Our group was dissolved, no longer "lovely hikers," no longer brothers and sisters of the trail. We were free to be individuals again, but we weren't quite ready to.

"I love each and every one of you," Celeste said, choking back tears. Real tears, not an act.

"You're a right good lot. Aren't they Liam?"

"Proper."

"I learned from all of you," Abe told us.

"We have a guest home in Colorado."

"We should do this again! All of us. We could climb Kilimanjaro together!"

"Yes!" cried a girl from Alabama.

"What do you say Joel?" Clint asked me.

"Sounds good," I nodded and smiled a very small smile. It was the truth. It sounded good. We both knew it would never happen. We shook hands.

"Let me go woman." Ed said to Celeste who was hugging him. "I'm not dying."

"But you..."

"You are too. We all are. So live young lady."

"So..." One of the girls from Alabama pulled me aside. "I still don't really know what Machu Picchu is. I mean, do you?"

"Well... It's a wonder."

"Yeah." We stood there awkwardly. As with all millennials an awkward pause caused her to reach for her cellphone. "Want to take a selfie?"

"Um, sure."

So she held up her camera and got a really great shot of the two of us standing in front of Machu Picchu, whatever in the heck it was.

"OMG, I look cute!"

ABOUT THE AUTHOR

Joel Paul Reisig

Former standup comedian turned author Joel Paul Reisig has worked as a wrangler, driven in a demolition derby, competed in the longest kayak race in the world, boxed in the Golden Gloves, ridden bulls and wrestled alligators, and raced a dog sled ninety miles across Michigan's frozen upper peninsula. He invites you to come on his next adventure with him, and promises you that you will laugh every step of the way.

BOOKS BY THIS AUTHOR

Midnight Run: One Comedian, Eight Sled Dogs.

In the hilarious new travelogue by Joel Paul Reisig, the author has a heart attack and is dumped by the women he loves. He decides to move to Michigan's frozen Upper Peninsula where he lives with an old musher, a moron, and forty-seven sled dogs, races in the Midnight Run, and falls for a girl who conveniently has the same name as the girl he lost!

"Authentic and funny. Joel nails a rookie's blunders and achievements on the trail with sled dogs"
   -Jeff King, four-time Iditarod champion

I Just Want Dry Underpants: An Average Joel Enters The World's Longest Kayak Race

In the hilarious new travelogue from Joel Paul Reisig "our generations Bill Bryson", the standup comedian turned adventure travel writer heads to Missouri and enters the world's longest kayak race, 340 nonstop miles across the entire state! Over the course of 77 hours of racing, Joel meets The Tan Man, a women with purple hair, a pastor, an Army colonel, a beer guzzling moron, a man with a baboon's heart, an eighty year old river dog, a college professor, and other colorful characters all crazy enough to take part in the toughest ultra-marathon on water! Joel strives to bring you into the boat with him as he paddles for three plus days – learning, laughing, and hallucinating! (Please feel free to wear dry underpants while reading this book).

Printed in Great Britain
by Amazon

18699484R00082